Ovid: A Very Short Introduction

VERY SHORT INTRODUCTIONS are for anyone wanting a stimulating and accessible way into a new subject. They are written by experts, and have been translated into more than 45 different languages.

The series began in 1995, and now covers a wide variety of topics in every discipline. The VSI library currently contains over 650 volumes—a Very Short Introduction to everything from Psychology and Philosophy of Science to American History and Relativity—and continues to grow in every subject area.

Very Short Introductions available now:

Available soon:

For more information visit our website

www.oup.com/vsi/

Llewelyn Morgan

OVID

A Very Short Introduction

OXFORD
UNIVERSITY PRESS

OXFORD
UNIVERSITY PRESS

Great Clarendon Street, Oxford, OX2 6DP,
United Kingdom

Oxford University Press is a department of the University of Oxford.
It furthers the University's objective of excellence in research, scholarship,
and education by publishing worldwide. Oxford is a registered trade mark of
Oxford University Press in the UK and in certain other countries

First edition published in 2020

Impression: 3

Published in the United States of America by Oxford University Press
198 Madison Avenue, New York, NY 10016, United States of America

British Library Cataloguing in Publication Data
Data available

Library of Congress Control Number: 2020938633

ISBN 978-0-19-883768-8

Printed in Great Britain by
Ashford Colour Press Ltd, Gosport, Hampshire

Links to third party websites are provided by Oxford in good faith and
for information only. Oxford disclaims any responsibility for the materials
contained in any third party website referenced in this work.

For Tom, QPR fanatic
medio tutissimus ibis

Contents

Acknowledgements

Over a professional life researching Ovid I have incurred countless debts. But I owe immediate thanks for help in writing this book to Ed Bispham, Seb Hyams, Matthew Robinson, Sophie Hay, Chris Tudor, Georgy Kantor, Alexandru Avram, Ida Östenberg, Maria Czepiel, Gail Trimble, Steve Heyworth, and Andrew Sillett. The readers for OUP offered excellent advice, and would all of them certainly have written a better Very Short Introduction to Ovid than I have. Above all I have been exceedingly fortunate in my OUP editors, Andrea Keegan, Jenny Nugee, and Luciana O'Flaherty, who have been more sympathetic than I deserve to my repeated requests for an extension, and expert at guiding me how to set about introducing to the wider world this scintillating Roman poet.

List of illustrations

Ovid

Chapter 1
Introduction: P. Ovidius Naso

Vivam!

So ends Ovid's masterpiece, the fifteen-book *Metamorphoses*: 'I shall live on!' The meandering timeline of this hugely influential poem has at long last reached the present day, and the poet celebrates the rise to power of the Caesars, Julius Caesar and his adoptive son and heir, Augustus. But it is with Ovid's own achievement that the poem concludes (15.871–9):

> Now I have brought to completion a work that neither Jove's wrath,
>> nor fire,
> nor sword, nor devouring age will have the power to efface.
> When it wishes, let that day which has jurisdiction over nothing
> but this body, put an end to the span of my uncertain years—
> still in the better part of me I shall pass immortal beyond
> the lofty stars, and my name will be imperishable,
> and as far as Roman might extends over the conquered world
> I shall be spoken on the lips of the people, and through all ages in
>> high repute,
> if the prophecies of bards contain any truth, I shall live on!

Given that we are still reading the *Metamorphoses* two millennia after Ovid's death, this can count as a remarkably accurate prophecy. What is more, no Greek or Roman poet is as accessible today as Ovid, to artists, writers, or the general reader, or has ever been in the intervening years—for if Ovid can seem at times to us in the 21st century a compellingly modern and contemporary voice, so he did in the 16th, 12th, and back in the 1st.

Which is not to suggest that Ovid's poetry is easy. A mistake first-time readers often make is to assume that his comparatively straightforward Latin reflects straightforward poetic thought. In fact Ovid is the most sophisticated and self-aware artist in a tradition of Latin verse, indebted in turn to Greek poetry, that foregrounds those qualities. Nor can it be claimed that Ovid's poetry has met with an exclusively uncritical press. In poetry and in life Ovid courted controversy, which both brought him celebrity and contributed to the banishment from Rome that he suffered at the height of his popularity. Some believe that the epilogue to the *Metamorphoses* was written in exile, and the idea that his 'better part' consisted in the verse that would survive him certainly resonates with the anguished ruminations of the ageing, exiled poet on poetry that had contributed to his misfortune, but remained his greatest consolation. Enthusiastic acceptance and equally vehement rejection have been the story of his reception, too. 'The sweet, witty soul of Ovid' that Francis Meres in *Palladis Tamia, Wits Treasury* (1598) identified 'in mellifluous and honey-tongued Shakespeare' is one side of this afterlife; John Dryden's distaste for Narcissus' soliloquy in *Metamorphoses* 3 in *Fables Ancient and Modern* (1700), its self-indulgent 'boyisms' so inferior to Chaucer, is another, equally representative. The Drydens have their place in this story, even as we emphasize the sweetness and wit.

Where Meres and Dryden might agree is that Ovid was a man, and a poet, constitutionally incapable of resisting a good joke.

Publius Ovidius Naso ('Naso' indicates an ancestor with a prominent nose) was born on the second day of the Quinquatrus, a festival of the goddess Minerva, in the consulship of Gaius Pansa and Aulus Hirtius—in more familiar terms, 20 March, 43 BCE. The Ovidii were *domi nobiles*, local elite, an ancient family (as Ovid asserts and surviving inscriptions confirm) from Sulmo, a town set in a fertile intermontane basin in the Apennine mountains east of Rome. Sulmona, as it is known today, was one of the leading towns of the Paeligni, a people of central Italy who in the days of Ovid's grandparents had gone to war against Rome, 'driven to honourable arms by their love of freedom' (*Amores* 3.15.9). This war between Rome and its erstwhile Italian allies (the 'Social War', 91–88 BCE) was a catalyst, paradoxically, for accelerated unification of the peoples of the Italian peninsula, a process which Augustus, the first emperor of Rome, was eager to take the credit for fostering and completing. By Ovid's time, a native of Italy was also by definition a Roman citizen, and powerful Italian families like Ovid's had been absorbed into the Roman ruling classes. Had he followed a conventional Roman script, Ovid himself could have represented a culmination of this development, the first Paelignian member of the Roman Senate.

This was certainly the ambition of Ovid's father. Alongside his brother, exactly a year his senior, Ovid was groomed for a public career, studying rhetoric in Rome and in Athens, a city past its glory days but still a centre for education. But while his brother showed a bent for oratory and the law, Ovid's was always for poetry. Obedient to his father, and further motivated by his brother's premature death when Ovid was 19, he dutifully took the first steps on a political career, holding two minor magistracies, the second of which was certainly of a judicial character and opened the way toward the Senate. He also acted as an arbitrator of private suits, a role that might indicate a reputation for competence. In the *Remedia Amoris* ('Cures for Love') he seems to offer a glimpse of his legal career when he recalls representing a husband in divorce proceedings, which the husband abruptly drops when he sets eyes upon his wife again (661–70).

But it was no good, the Muses would not let go: 'I was affected by my father's words, and leaving Helicon wholly behind me | I attempted to write words freed from metre. | But of its own volition song found its fitting rhythm, | and whatever I tried to say was verse' (*Tristia* 4.10.23–6). That account comes from an autobiographical poem that Ovid wrote late in life. 'The Senate House awaited me, but I reduced the width of my stripe', he continues—he replaced a tunic bearing a broad purple stripe, indicating senatorial ambitions, with the narrow parallel stripes of the lesser, equestrian social order.

As early as his late teens Ovid had begun to make a name for himself as a poet, and his autobiography moves on from his abortive public career to the literary scene of his youth. Propertius was the author of love poetry that Ovid would imitate in his first collection, the *Amores*, and Q. Horatius Flaccus, or Horace, was the composer of one of the most celebrated achievements of Roman literature, the lyric poems known as the *Odes*. Both seem to have been close acquaintances of the precocious Naso. But 'Virgil I only saw', *Vergilium uidi tantum*—the greatest poet in a remarkable flowering of literature under Augustus, Virgil was the author of the epic *Aeneid*, a celebration of Rome's and Augustus' right to rule. The most significant cultural achievement of the Augustan age, the *Aeneid* also reset Roman literature: no poet thereafter could ignore it, as Ovid's wistful reminiscence implies. Virgil was thirty years older than Ovid, shy and reclusive: he died in 19 BCE. Tibullus, another love poet, died in the same year, too early, Ovid says, for them to be friends (*Amores* 3.9 is Ovid's poem-long lament for him).

All these poets are conventionally described by scholars as Augustan poets. In truth, though, much of Virgil's and Horace's poetry was written before Augustus ended years of conflict, and secured control of Rome, by defeating Mark Antony and Cleopatra in 31–30 BCE. Their masterpieces, the *Aeneid* and the *Odes*, were written early in Augustus' reign, and both works are still intensely exercised by what had gone before, the civil wars that the historian Tacitus called 'unbroken strife for twenty years, no custom, no law' (*Annals* 3.28). Ovid's life, in contrast, had begun in upheaval, both the consuls in his birth year, Hirtius and Pansa, dying during their tenure, casualties of the violence that had followed Julius Caesar's assassination in 44 BCE. But the mature Ovid, coming of age in the early 20s BCE, never experienced the crisis to which Augustus and everything he entailed—restrictions on freedom, greater surveillance of private lives—were, for writers such as Horace and Virgil, a necessary response. Ovid's poetic career began shortly after Augustus assumed that honorific name in 27 BCE (he had previously gone by the name of his adoptive father, C. Julius Caesar), and he died three or four years after the emperor. In that sense, and in the pleasure and inspiration he drew from the thriving, peaceful city over which Augustus presided, Ovid is the most Augustan of the Augustan poets. But this most Augustan poet, who had never really known anything but the *pax Augusta*, also had the least emotional investment in Augustus' achievement, and it shows.

Ovid's poetic career is clear enough in outline, at least. The order of composition generally assumed is *Amores* ('Loves'), (single) *Heroides* ('Heroines'), *Ars Amatoria* ('Art of Love'), *Remedia Amoris* ('Cures for Love'), *Metamorphoses* ('Transformations'), *Fasti* ('Calendar'), *Tristia* ('Sad poems'), *Ibis* ('Ibis', the bird), *Epistulae ex Ponto* 1–4 ('Letters from the Black Sea'), and (double) *Heroides*. Poems were rewritten, or written simultaneously, to disrupt this tidy consecutive list, of course, and Ovid also wrote poetry which now only survives in fragments. The *Phaenomena*, probably juvenilia, was a translation of a poem on constellations by the unaccountably popular Hellenistic poet Aratus (3rd century BCE), something on which young Roman poets were in the habit of cutting their teeth. *Medea*, a tragic drama, fell between a second edition of the *Amores* and the *Ars Amatoria*, and proved, so the later critic Quintilian (*c.*35–*c.*100 CE) reckoned, what heights Ovid could have attained 'if he had been willing to direct his talent, not indulge it' (10.1.98)—but Quintilian, it is fair to say, had no sense of humour. The 'Cosmetics for the Female Face', *Medicamina Faciei Femineae*, was apparently a dry run for the *Ars Amatoria*, its failure to survive in full no doubt a result of the success of the latter poem; and there were short epigrams. Another possibility emerged from an archaeological dig in the vicinity of Sulmona. Excavations of the sanctuary of Hercules Curinus on the slopes of Monte Morrone (see Figure 1), traditionally identified as Ovid's villa, were begun in 1957, the bimillennium of Ovid's birth. One intriguing discovery was a pillar bearing ancient graffiti including twelve lines of poetry with *NASONIS*, 'by Ovid', inscribed above them: the verses, only partly legible, do not correspond to any of his surviving works.

These lines may or may not be 'by Ovid', but there are certainly other cases where the mystique of Ovid's name has attracted poems to it that we don't believe he wrote. An example will show how freely attributions floated about in antiquity, and illustrate the fundamental paucity of information that modern scholars have to contend with. A fragment of the *Halieutica*, a poem on sea-fishing, would not be associated with Ovid at all if it weren't for Pliny the Elder, who cites the poem and attributes it to Ovid in his encyclopedic *Natural History*. Pliny was writing only sixty years or so after Ovid's death, but it is surprising how quickly accurate knowledge of poets, as opposed to their poetry, could be lost: similarly unlikely things are being attributed to Virgil shortly after. Information persists in Graeco-Roman antiquity if it is written down, essentially, and that is more likely to happen to great poetry than the mundane details of a poet's life. Thus, while Ovid's poetry largely survives, basic biographical information is lost to us, and we owe what we do know about Ovid largely to his own reminiscences. Suetonius a century later effectively invented the genre of biography, and wrote lives of poets among others, but we don't know whether he ever wrote a life of Ovid, and if he did it doesn't survive.

1. The site of the shrine of Hercules at Monte Morrone, looking south toward Sulmona.

A factor specific to Ovid, however, is his circumstances at the end of his life, which is when Pliny believed he wrote the *Halieutica* (32.152). Whatever Augustus' intention in banishing Ovid, it had the effect, in a culture enjoying only very rudimentary communication technology, of making the poet disappear from sight. Ovid's own poetry from exile was in large part an effort to counteract his invisibility in Rome, but it remains the case that remarkably little information survives in ancient sources about the final years of a man who had been the most fêted writer in Rome. Between Ovid's death in 17 or 18 CE and a notice of his death in St Jerome's *Chronicon* (381 CE), a chronology of events from Adam to his own day, we have just one isolated reference to Ovid's exile in a poem by Statius at the end of the 1st century CE, and even here the allusion is really to the poetry that Ovid had sent back to Rome.

Jerome's notice against the year 17 nevertheless reminds us of one of the most important facts about this author, though we're not entirely confident even here of the precise date: 'The poet Ovid died in exile, and is buried near the town of Tomis.' Aside from Ovid's deathdate, 17 or maybe 18, we have just a skeletal framework of absolute dates to set his career within—birth in 43 BCE, his brother's death in 24 BCE, references in the *Ars Amatoria* and *Remedia Amoris* to events that place those poems securely between 1 BCE and 2 CE, and his exile in 8 or 9 CE.

Hard to date precisely it may be, but Ovid's poetry makes good sense as an oeuvre. One thing that binds his rich and diverse body of work together is a restless commitment to innovation. Exhausting the possibilities of love-elegy (*Amores*), he wrote a lover's guide (*Ars Amatoria*), a brilliant reinvention of love-elegy in a new guise, and then capped that with a guide to falling out of love (*Remedia Amoris*); letters from abandoned mythical heroines (the single *Heroides*) were followed (some time later) by exchanges of letters between mythical lovers; above all, in the

Metamorphoses, love poetry was not so much abandoned as reimagined as epic plot. Ovid was famous, indeed notorious, for his *ingenium*, his inspiration or native wit, but these innovations also tell us how popular his poetry was, how successful he was in finding a readership that demanded ever more from him.

By the time of the *Ars Amatoria*, furthermore, Virgil, Propertius, and Horace were all dead, and Ovid had the stage effectively to himself, the dominant cultural voice of his day—with one fatal exception, Augustus. The emperor had his narrative, of national renewal driven by moral discipline and respect for the past, and it was a potent one. As for Ovid, a disapproving contemporary complained how he 'filled this age with amatory arts and ideas' (L. Cestius Pius quoted by Seneca the Elder, *Controversiae* 3.7): the story that Ovid told had its own seductive power, but it was at persistent, albeit subtle, variance with Augustus', and this was an irritant for which the emperor's patience would not prove to be limitless.

My term 'innovation' here needs some clarification. Ovid was a radical spirit within a deeply conservative literary culture. Each of Ovid's new departures is actually a twist on established convention: for example his *Amores* plays inventively with the rules of a genre (or sub-genre), love-elegy, established and refined by predecessors such as Propertius and Cornelius Gallus, while the *Metamorphoses* is an exuberantly unorthodox epic which only works as such if the pre-existing 'rules' of the form are understood. This poetry is intensely aware of its predecessors, as objects of both respect and rivalry, and reminiscences of earlier poetry (referred to as 'allusion') are not only common but essential means of expression. This style of poetry has been neatly encapsulated as 'creative imitation'. Its imitative character diminishes the power of this poetry not a whit, I should insist—indeed, I would propose that there can only be true originality in the presence of established rules, and the traditional character of Graeco-Roman literature merely acknowledges that truth.

9

A name that will feature regularly in this book is Callimachus, a Greek poet active in Alexandria, the capital of Greek Egypt, in the 3rd century BCE, and associated with the famous Library of Alexandria (within the original 'Museum', a kind of ancient research centre), who exerted a huge influence over Roman poetry from its earliest days. His most celebrated poem, the *Aetia* ('Causes'), only survives for us in fragments, most of them on papyri discovered in Egypt at the turn of the 19th and 20th centuries. In a series of narratives the *Aetia* had explained the origins of peculiar rituals, practices, and artefacts across the Greek world and beyond (the first Roman to appear in Greek literature featured in one of Callimachus' stories). In Ovid's oeuvre the *Fasti*, his poetic calendar, bears a particularly close resemblance to the *Aetia*, as we shall see, but in this poem and elsewhere Callimachus had expressed strong opinions on poetry in memorable ways, and his imagery of pure fountains, slender Muses, and untrodden roads was much exploited in Roman poetic manifestos.

Whether those Roman poets understood Callimachus' pronouncements exactly as he had intended them is less certain, but he came to represent for them a cluster of literary principles which had formative importance in the literature of this period. Those principles include: an emphasis on writing over performance; an intellectual and self-aware approach to composition which reflected Callimachus' real-life role as an academic at the Museum (literally 'Temple of the Muses'), familiar with the long history of Greek literature; a preference for brevity over length, indistinguishable from a rejection of higher forms of poetry, epic especially, in favour of humbler genres and subject matter; and a promotion of an individual perspective, a first-person narrator, over the omniscient, impersonal narrative conventional in more elevated genres. The essential affinity between Callimachean and Roman poetics lay perhaps in a shared 'belatedness'—Callimachus a Greek poet sensitive to his late appearance in a glorious tradition of literary achievement, while Roman poets bore the burden of both their own native literature and the Greek literature before it, a daunting challenge to their own creative abilities.

Callimachean poetry, sometimes also called 'Hellenistic' (a word evoking the vastly expanded Greek world after the conquests of Alexander the Great, and its wealthy urban centres), was inherently elitist poetry. A well-read poet wrote for comparably sophisticated readers, and thereby reduced his natural readership to a very restricted slice of ancient society. 'Publishing' books in Rome was a matter of making one's work available to be copied. There were commercial booksellers, but much of this copying will have been done privately, with circulation primarily among Ovid's acquaintances within literary society. Poets also shared some of their poetry in recitations, another select gathering to which the great and good might be invited; and a new phenomenon at Rome in Ovid's day was public libraries, from which he tells us that his poetry from exile was excluded; another source informs us, with some poignancy, that Ovid was a close friend of the man in charge of the great library established by Augustus on the Palatine hill, C. Julius Hyginus (Suetonius, *Gramm.* 20). There is some evidence that Ovid's poetry penetrated deeper into Roman society than most poetry did: Ovid himself refers to performances of (probably) his *Heroides* on stage, featuring an element of dancing, and these would have widened his audience significantly. But it remains the case that the target audience of this poetry is narrow, and the literature itself evidence of how the Roman upper classes policed access to their charmed circle. The cultural capital required to play the literary games that this poetry typically involves, the knowledge of Greek language and literature, art, and philosophy that it demands, is immense. At the same time, what its socio-economic origins ensure is poetry of unparalleled sophistication. Two thousand years old it may be, but we can banish from our minds any thought that it might be primitive.

A final respect in which Callimachus was an important model for Ovid is metrical. Poetry is simply not poetry in this literary culture unless it observes a set metrical system, in Graeco-Roman antiquity essentially a matter of the number and length (long or short) of syllables. When Ovid describes how he tried to do legal prose, but it always came out as verse, 'prose' is 'words freed from metres', and classical metre can to the uninitiated seem an arbitrary straitjacket for poetry to adopt. But as with the generic conventions we have already glimpsed, a poet like Ovid can achieve meaning by manipulating established metrical practice, and can do so partly because in Graeco-Roman antiquity genre and metre were closely associated. The two metrical systems relevant to Ovid are the so-called dactylic hexameter, which was the vehicle for epics such as Homer's *Iliad* and Virgil's *Aeneid* and consequently known as the 'heroic metre' by the ancients; and the elegiac couplet (the metre of all Ovid's surviving poems bar the *Metamorphoses*), which combined a dactylic hexameter with a line known as a dactylic pentameter (the name implying it was slightly shorter). Elegiac metre thus shared an essential kinship with heroic verse, the hexameter that opened every couplet, but was also fundamentally unlike it by virtue of the pentameter that followed, and that enshrined in the very form of most of Ovid's poetry an antagonistic relationship with epic poetry.

Callimachus' own metrical practice reinforced this status of elegy, the poetry composed in elegiac couplets, as a rival to hexametrical epic. The Greek poet had composed freely in hexameters and elegiacs, but the work for which he was most celebrated, the *Aetia*, was in elegiacs, and he thus came to be considered a champion of elegiac poetry, and 'elegiac' as a term more or less synonymous with 'Callimachean' as a description of his characteristic style of poetry, its preferences in content as well as its fundamental rejection of epic, the higher form associated with the hexameter. In the *Remedia Amoris* Ovid discusses metrical proprieties, explaining which topics are suited to which metres (381–2): 'Achilles must not be spoken of in the metre of Callimachus', he insists, 'and Cydippe is not a topic for your mouth, Homer.' Cydippe is a character from the *Aetia* we will meet again in Ovid's

Heroides, while Achilles is the protagonist of Homer's epic (and hexametrical) *Iliad*. Elegiacs are thus defined as Callimachus' trademark form, the heroic hexameter as Homer's; but in addition Cydippe's elegiac treatment is a love story that explains an antiquarian puzzle, while Achilles in the *Iliad* is a tale of war.

It is worth mentioning here an older association with mourning and lament that clung to the elegiac metre and surfaces periodically in Ovid's poetry—in his lament for his fellow poet Tibullus in *Amores* 3.9, for example. An illustration of the attention given to metres in their own right is an analysis of the elegiac couplet by a scholar contemporary with Ovid, Didymus Chalcenterus ('Didymus Brazenguts', so called in reference to his astonishingly prolific output, vanishingly little of which survives). Didymus located the aptitude of elegy for lament in the very structure of the verse: the shorter pentameter line that follows the (epic) hexameter in every couplet, he wrote, 'does not keep pace with the vigour of the first line, but seems to expire and be extinguished along with the fortunes of the dead man'. The hexameter embodies human success, in other words, and the pentameter human misfortune. Other analyses of elegiac metre coexisted with Didymus', and elegy is associated with much more than just mournful poetry, but what was agreed in antiquity was that the essential character of poetic genres was immanent in their preferred metrical vehicles.

As an individual poet, Ovid of course had his own idiosyncrasies, and ancient and modern critics have had much to say about them. Dryden's irritation with Ovid's 'boyisms', for example, has a long history. Seneca the Younger in his *Natural Questions* quotes Ovid's account of the Flood in the first book of the *Metamorphoses*, then chastises the poet for reducing such a momentous subject to 'schoolboy silliness' when he illustrates the effects of the flood with a wolf swimming among sheep and the waves carrying off lions (3.27.13–15). Ovid is *ingeniosissimus*, 'supremely inventive', according to Seneca, but he also seems to agree with Quintilian that he is 'too fond of his own talent (*ingenium*)' (10.1.89).

This perception of Ovid as an abundantly talented writer who lacked self-discipline is also present in the richest source of information we have about Ovid's youth aside from his own account, the reminiscences of Seneca the Elder (so called to distinguish him from the son I've just quoted) about the declamatory culture of his own youth. Declamation was a training exercise for aspirant orators, thus a prerequisite of the political and legal career for which Ovid had been destined. He features in Seneca's recollections as a talented, if wilful, declaimer who 'was in the habit of running through the commonplaces in no fixed order' (*Contr.* 2.2.9), but was still more disciplined in his declamation than his poetry, where 'he was not unaware of his faults, but in love with them' (2.2.12). There follows a delightful anecdote describing how Ovid's friends begged him to let them delete three of his most egregiously self-indulgent lines, and Ovid asked to exempt his three favourites; when they came to compare notes, the two lists were identical. One of the lines was Ovid's description of the Minotaur, and you can see both points of view: *semibouemque uirum semiuirumque bouem*, 'the half-bull man and half-man bull' (*Ars Amatoria* 2.24). Seneca continues: 'From this it is clear that this extremely talented man (*summi ingenii uir*) lacked not the judgement but the will to restrain the indiscipline of his own poems. He was in the habit of saying from time to time that a face was more attractive if it had some blemish on it.'

For our purposes, however, the most interesting implication of Ovid's prominence in Seneca's account is what it conveys about Ovid's cultural milieu, and crucially also about the tastes, expectations, and aesthetics of his target readership. Declamation was training for real oratory in court, but dealt in fictional or distantly historical scenarios (advising the long-dead dictator Sulla whether to retire or not, for example). On the evidence of

Seneca, especially, it tended to promote eye-catching turns of phrase at the price of anything more practical. A description of declamation as 'loud, empty witticisms', *sententiarum uanissimus strepitus* (Petronius, *Satyricon* 1), gives a taste of a training exercise significantly removed from the reality of persuasive oratory. Ovid himself disliked the more legalistic types of declamation, Seneca informs us, so it was perhaps even more the case with him that declamation was a training in sheer rhetorical invention, the skill of speaking engagingly to any given circumstance, a strictly artificial exercise in verbal dexterity. It is telling also how regular a point of reference Ovid's poetry is in Seneca's discussion of declamatory practice—the practices of declamation and poetry could get very close indeed. 'His speech even then could be regarded as simply poetry in prose', Seneca comments on Ovid's style of oratory (*Contr.* 2.2.8).

So when critics tell Ovid off for being too indulgent of his own *ingenium*, they are indeed identifying something characteristic of him, but it is also something that his contemporaries, and likely first readers, might well have been inclined to value. Would those Roman readers have objected, as Dryden did, to Narcissus' lengthy contemplation of his paradoxical circumstances in the *Metamorphoses*, passionately in love with his own reflection, including the brilliant/outrageous paradox *inopem me copia fecit*, 'Abundance has left me destitute', or would that actually have been one of the things they most cherished in this poet? To propose that Ovid is writing primarily for lawyers would be unforgivably glib, no doubt, but it may not be entirely lacking in explanatory power.

Finally, a word on Ovid's private life. For reasons given, details of a poet's life are scarce unless authors are generous enough to tell us themselves. Furthermore, Graeco-Roman poetry is rarely confessional, even at times when it appears to be: the real, historical circumstances of the poet are seldom the poetry's main concern. In Ovid's case the poet's misfortune is our good luck, as his exile caused him to reflect deeply on his past life in Rome. From *Tristia* 4.10 especially, a brief but invaluable poetic autobiography, we learn that he was married three times, the first two marriages ending in divorce (not uncommon in the Roman elite). By his second marriage he had a daughter, herself twice married, and two grandchildren; a stepdaughter by his third marriage is apparently the addressee, under the name 'Perilla', of one of his most celebrated poems from exile, *Tristia* 3.7, while her husband, P. Suillius Rufus, is the recipient of one of his *Letters from the Black Sea* (4.8): Suillius' later career was chequered, to say the least, but both he and his son, Ovid's step-grandchild M. Suillius Nerullinus, rose to the consulship, the highest political office in Rome.

In both cases that was long after Ovid's death, but the distinctions achieved by his relatives hint at Ovid's high social status, in which respect he was quite different from a poet like Horace, for example. This emerges most clearly from *Letters from the Black Sea*, where named connections in Rome are addressed in the hopes they might facilitate his return. We can, if we choose, discern from that and other sources a fairly conventional life among the Roman elite before his banishment—networking with the high nobility, marrying a wealthy and well-connected third wife (none of his wives are ever named), and all the other activities of a typical socially elevated Roman male energetically cultivating his name and status. His third wife, who remained in Rome at his exile, had been associated with Marcia, for example, a first cousin of Augustus whom we will meet again at the end of the *Fasti*, while an important supporter of the young Ovid's poetry was M. Valerius Messalla Corvinus, soldier, orator, author, and patron who was one of the most prominent figures of Augustan Rome. None of these contacts was any use in persuading Augustus or Tiberius to recall him from exile, sadly.

We owe the phrase 'in a nutshell' to the Romans, not to Ovid but the orator Cicero, who described a text of Homer's *Iliad* written in lettering so tiny it could be enclosed in a nut (*in nuce*: Pliny the Elder, *Natural History* 7.85). The conceit hangs not just on the length of the epic *Iliad* but on Homer's status as the greatest poet there ever had been and ever could be, a figure it was unfeasible to contain within so restricted a space. This is an assessment of Homer that Ovid would undoubtedly have endorsed. But it could be argued that Ovid's legacy, the profound debt owed him by literature and art, is even greater than Homer's, so it may yet be a sound analogy for the challenge that faces me in this Very Short Introduction. (We are not told whether anyone could actually *read* the Homer-in-a-nutshell.) I cannot avoid being radically selective, but the task is to communicate the creativity and wit of a great Roman poet, and explain thereby the inspiration he has provided to authors and artists ever since.

Chapter 2
Love poetry

'Elegy admits that it owes as much to me, | as noble Epic owes to Virgil,' Ovid boasts in one of the poems we'll consider in this chapter, the *Remedia Amoris*, asserting his equality with the most renowned poet of recent times as well as his allegiance to a rival poetic tradition. Virgil's *Aeneid* was a rewriting of the Homeric epics, the *Iliad* and *Odyssey*, for a Roman audience, and a constant point of reference for the younger poet. 'Elegy' here denotes a metrical form first and foremost, as we noted in Chapter 1—the elegiac couplet which combined the heroic hexameter with a shorter length. But implied also is the subject matter associated with that form, poetry that was lighter than epic, and cleverer. In Rome the most successful example of elegiac verse was a variety of love poetry known to modern scholars as love-elegy, and it is with Ovid's ventures in this sub-genre that this chapter will be concerned, his three books of *Amores*, 'Loves', and the further development of love-elegy represented by the *Ars Amatoria* ('Art of Love') and *Remedia Amoris* ('Cures for Love').

Ovid seems to have been composing love-elegy from as early as his late teens, and while the *Amores* are not the first poetry that we think he wrote, they are what established his reputation. More than that, the *Amores* set the terms for the rest of Ovid's poetic career, marking him out as the leading proponent of elegiac verse, with everything that might entail. A combative relationship with the higher genre of epic was one thing that elegy brought with it, and Ovid's relationship with Virgil's poetry was one of rivalry as well as respect. It may be significant that in the elegiac couplet with which I began this chapter Ovid gives his own achievement the place of honour in the epic hexameter, subordinating Virgil's to the shorter, less prestigious pentameter.

Roman love-elegy owes a debt to a tradition of Greek erotic epigrams as well as to Greek and Roman comedy and the related theatrical genre of mime, but unlike most Roman poetic forms it had no direct Greek model. Ovid's immediate points of reference are Tibullus and Propertius, older contemporaries and the latter an acquaintance, but the inventor of love-elegy had been a friend and contemporary of Virgil in the previous generation, Cornelius Gallus, a soldier-poet who took his own life in 26 BCE after falling foul of the emperor Augustus. 'Tibullus was your successor, Gallus, and Propertius his,' Ovid writes (*Tristia* 4.10.53–4), 'Fourth after these was I myself in time's order.' To Gallus we can credit the quite rigid conventions of love-elegy: poems recount the tribulations of a male lover, identified with the poet, pursuing an unequal affair with a capricious female love interest.

The three-book edition of the *Amores* that has come down to us, as Ovid himself informs us in a prefatory epigram, is an abridged version of what had originally been five books, presumably issued consecutively between around 25 BCE (when Ovid himself was 18 or so) and 15 BCE. When exactly the new, trim, three-book edition saw the light of day is anyone's guess (as indeed is the reason for this abbreviated edition), but it was perhaps shortly before he started work on the *Ars Amatoria* in about 1 BCE. The latter poem, an inspired twist on love-elegy that claims to use the poet's hard-earned expertise to teach the art of love to others, was originally in two books instructing men how to achieve success in love. The *Ars* clearly enjoyed instant success, and was quickly supplemented by a third book aimed at women, and then the *Remedia Amoris* that cured anyone who'd been rash enough to follow his initial advice.

As the young poet composed his witty, flippant love poetry, Augustus was successfully stabilizing Rome after the trauma of the Civil Wars, transforming the city's architecture, enacting moral legislation, and staging a religious festival celebrating new beginnings—but these developments are reflected only very obliquely in the *Amores*. The issue of the realism of Ovid's love poetry is not a simple one, as we shall see, but what is certainly true is that the poems of the *Amores*, though they claim to document the poet's troubled love life, offer something much more artificial. Ovid's lover is called Corinna, but is heavily fictionalized if not fully fictional; and the poet describes his life in terms of a series of highly conventional scenarios inherited from the short but intense tradition of love-elegy that had preceded him. Like all Roman poetry, furthermore, the *Amores* is acutely conscious of its position in literary history, and no Roman poet is more interested in his own status as a poet than Ovid is. The *Amores* is thus less poetry about love than poetry about love poetry, its primary appeal lying not in impassioned expressions of affection but witty manipulation of poetic convention. We should not overstate Ovid's originality here: Propertius' first poem explains how he'd squandered a whole year in his infatuation for his lover Cynthia, but also conveys, by implication, both his debt to Cornelius Gallus and his determination to rival his predecessor's achievement. Love-elegy was a thoroughly self-conscious poetic form from its inception, in other words. But the strictly literary motivations are more implicit in Propertius' writing than in Ovid's, no matter how formative we may in fact suspect them to be. It follows that a characteristic feature of Ovid's love poetry is its detachment and lightness of touch, amusing and diverting even when he claims to be experiencing bleak despair at Corinna's mistreatment of him.

Ovid's first readers would have been trained in the conventions of love-elegy by reading Propertius and Tibullus, and the four books of Cornelius Gallus' *Amores* which are represented for us now by just ten surviving lines (nine of them discovered on an island in Lake Nasser, Egypt in 1978). In lieu of that literary acculturation, let us devote a little time to an illustrative example of Ovid's love poetry. We are in the opening poem of his second book, and Ovid is explaining the genesis of the poems that follow. He had been writing an epic poem, he informs us, but then his girlfriend shut him out, at which point he was obliged to revert to love-elegy, because epic wouldn't help him persuade her to open the door.

But Ovid doesn't put it quite as simply as that (*Am.* 2.1.11–22):

> I had dared, I remember, to tell of the wars of Heaven
> and hundred-handed Gyges—and my voice was strong enough—
> the time when Earth took her disastrous revenge and, piled on
>   Olympus,
> steep Ossa bore the weight of sheer Pelion.
> In my hands I held the stormclouds, and the thunderbolt, and Jove,
> the thunderbolt he'd hurl in defence of his own Heaven.
> My beloved closed her door! I let fall the thunderbolt, and Jove:
> Jove himself dropped from my mind.
> Jove, pardon me! Your weapons were no use to me:
> that closed door was a thunderbolt stronger than yours.
> I have taken up again my proper weapons, my charming, light elegies:
> their gentle words have softened the hard door before.

The epic that Ovid had allegedly been in the process of writing has an archetypal plot, the defeat by Jupiter and the gods of an assault on Heaven by the rebellious Giants, the so-called Gigantomachy, a myth that depicted the imposition of order on chaos in the Universe. As such, it was favoured in self-promotion by political leaders (see Figure 2), and came also to represent a fundamental impulse of the epic genre, itself deeply concerned with political

2. Athena fighting the Giants, from a monument of the Attalid dynasty of Pergamum. The Gigantomachy symbolized the imposition of order on chaos, and here celebrates a monarch's victory over external enemies.

legitimacy. Thus the Gigantomachy is a persistent undercurrent in Virgil's *Aeneid*, informing his story of the divine project to bring the *pax Romana* to the world. Here, though, all the panoply of Heaven is not the slightest use to Ovid, so he's obliged to abandon it and write more love-elegy. The implication is that all the remaining poems of *Amores* Book 2 will be serenades sung by the shut-out lover to Corinna indoors.

Rebellious Giants can effectively stand for epic in its entirety: the Gigantomachy is an encapsulation of that genre. Closed doors fulfil the very same role for love-elegy. The scenario of the *exclusus amator*, 'shut-out lover', recurs constantly in Ovid's love poetry in one form or another, a similarly defining motif for love-elegy. Ovid thus stages in this opening poem an encounter of epic and elegy is their most abstract forms, and this is all, needless to say, far removed from 'a spontaneous overflow of powerful feelings' (as Wordsworth once described his poetic ideal). What the reader gets from this love poetry is the intellectual pleasure of delving the complex traditions in which this literary culture traded. It is hyper-sophisticated poetry, even too damn clever by half (the ancient critics of Ovid certainly thought so), but Ovid is always an appealing combination of the cerebral and the downright silly, and this account of (we need to remind ourselves) the poet's heartbreak is also extremely funny: epic's pompous self-image is reduced to Ovid balancing Jupiter, Father of the Gods, in the palm of his hand, and then abruptly dropping him.

The self-consciousness that we see in Ovid's love-elegy is, as already indicated, a feature associated with the Greek poet Callimachus, and equally true to Callimachus is the kind of self-definition against higher literary forms that we see in *Amores* 2.1, and more fundamentally the intellectual engagement of both writer and reader in the poetic exercise that this poetry requires. The very layout of elegiac books points in the same direction. Each of the three books of the *Amores* was, in its original form, like any other literature of this period, a separate book roll (in Latin a *uolumen*, hence 'volume', see Figure 5), and much could be intuited about the character of a poem, metre and actual content aside, from the relation of the poem to this book unit. Thus Virgil's *Aeneid* and Ovid's own *Metamorphoses*, both of which make a claim to epic status, do so not least by being single poems stretching across a plurality of books (the *Aeneid* filled twelve book rolls, the *Metamorphoses* fifteen). What Callimachus had championed, in contrast, was short, polished poetry, the product of the poet's meticulous application. In an epigram celebrating the 3rd-century BCE poet Aratus' influential poem *Phaenomena*, Callimachus had welcomed the 'delicate | phrases, the intense sleeplessness of Aratus' (*Epigram* 29.3–4), Aratus' lack of sleep being down both to the topic of the *Phaenomena*, the night sky, and the effort that Aratus had devoted to its composition, writing and rewriting his poetry into the small hours. Such Callimachean aesthetics are reflected in books of Ovid's *Amores* containing fifteen (or more) poems, each composition essentially unrelated to its neighbours: every one a small, perfectly formed, Callimachean work of art. But there is a restlessness about Ovid's Callimacheanism: if Callimachus stood for the new and unpredictable, it is an equally Callimachean gesture when Ovid introduces consecutive poems that prove unexpectedly to be related to one other, for example a pair of poems on a female slave of Corinna, Cypassis, *Amores* 2.7–8, which explore radically divergent perspectives on a dispute between the poet and his lover.

The continuity and discontinuity of poetic compositions, whether they run on for book after book like Virgil's *Aeneid*, or finish after seventy lines like a typical poem of Ovid's *Amores*, is thus one way in which the contest between epic and Callimachean poetry, this fundamental concern of Augustan poetry, was pursued, and it will be especially relevant when we consider the literary manifestos, explicit and implicit, of Ovid's *Metamorphoses* and *Fasti*. But the character of larger elegiac or epic compositions could also be read into the metrical vehicles they favoured, the dactylic hexameter of epic lending itself naturally to extended narratives, while elegiacs were apt to resolve themselves into self-contained couplets, thus producing a disjointed narrative style appropriate to shorter compositions—a tendency that Ovid worked to enhance. The individual Ovidian elegiac couplet is an achievement not to be ignored, thoughts wittily formulated within the narrow compass of two lines, exploiting the balanced structures of the form, and in Latin, once your eye is in, of crystalline clarity. Here, as an illustration of his seemingly effortless control of a challenging medium, is the poet complaining that Corinna's treachery leaves no outward mark (*Am.* 3.3.1–8):

esse deos, i, crede! fidem iurata fefellit,
    et facies illi, quae fuit ante, manet!
quam longos habuit nondum periura capillos,
    tam longos, postquam numina laesit, habet.

candida candorem roseo suffusa rubore
  ante fuit: niueo lucet in ore rubor.
pes erat exiguus: pedis est artissima forma.
  longa decensque fuit: longa decensque manet.

Believe there are gods, if you will: she swore and betrayed her oath,
  and her beauty remains as it was before!
As long as her hair was before she was forsworn,
  so long is it now that she has abused the gods.
She was fair, her fairness mixed with rosy red
  before, and red still glows on her snow-white face.
Her foot was small: most delicate still is the shape of her foot.
  Tall and graceful she was: tall and graceful she remains.

Highly formulaic elegy may have been as a literary form, but the behaviour attributed to themselves by the love-elegists was unconventional, indeed (if ever taken as an account of actual behaviour) positively scandalous in a Roman context. The male lovers courted humiliation at the hands of women who were of low social status, typically ex-slaves, but whom they described as *dominae*—'mistresses' in the sense of slave-owners—a shocking reversal of the conventional Roman view of the proper hierarchy of the sexes, and the fundamental value of free status. As love-elegy is wont to do, Ovid underlines the immorality of his alleged lifestyle, encouraging the disapproval of the reader: 'If there be anyone who think it shameful to be enslaved to a girl, | by his judgment I shall be convicted of shamefulness!' (*Am.* 2.17.1–2); 'Naso, poet of his own depravity', he calls himself elsewhere (*Am.* 2.1.2). And the contrast with a respectable life is regularly drawn: 'Why, gnawing Envy, do you cast at me my years of indolence, | and call my song the work of a useless wit, | complaining that, while vigorous youth attends me, I neither, | in the manner of our fathers, pursue the dusty rewards of warfare, | nor learn the long-winded laws, nor | have offered my voice for sale in the thankless forum?' (*Am.* 1.15.1–6). Here the conventional activities of elite young men at Rome, in the military and the law, are

Love poetry

25

contrasted with his poetic activity, but also with the feckless
lifestyle which that poetry purports to record.

A more succinct formulation comes in a poem addressed to an
author of epic poetry and close friend, Pompeius Macer, where
Ovid summarizes his subject matter, in conscious contrast to
Macer's, as '*indoor* achievements and *private* wars', *resque domi
gestas et mea bella* (2.18.12), ways of describing love affairs that
appropriate the public language of conventional male activity, *res
gestae* and *bella*, for a life devoted to private pleasures. If one did
not behave as a man should in Rome, furthermore, one did not
qualify as a proper man. Love-elegy controversially claims for
itself the epithet *mollis*, 'soft', as a description of the genre and its
protagonists, a word the Romans derived from *mulier*, 'woman',
and which defined a man as effeminate and sexually deviant. (The
'molly houses' of 18th- and 19th-century England appropriated in
comparable fashion the Latin word and its associations.)

Love-elegy had the potential, then, to be subversive and shocking.
But it is an elusive form in this respect. On the one hand Ovid is
writing in a poetic tradition, and an unusually rigid one at that: he
claims to be lying on Corinna's threshold begging for admittance
simply because that is what love-elegists do. On the other hand
love-elegy purports to be describing the poet's actual behaviour,
and includes on occasion powerfully authenticating notes. For
example, *Amores* 3.2 describes an attempted seduction in the
Circus Maximus on race day, where the rules of seating allowed
unrelated men and women to sit beside each other. The occasion
is a familiar Roman scene, and it is vividly evoked, for instance
when the statue of Venus, goddess of love, nods as she is carried in
the parade preceding the event, and the poet-lover affects to
interpret it as a sign he'll be successful. There is a psychological
plausibility here, too, the naive credulity that the poet-lover
attributes to himself, and it all helps to make the scenario credible.
The sequence of poems with which Book 1 opens impress on the
reader in a range of ways the artificiality of the poetic exercise,

only for Ovid to introduce Corinna in *Amores* 1.5 with a vivid and erotic vignette: *Aestus erat*, 'It was a summer day…'. Such occasional (and always, I should add, deniable) hints that a real lifestyle might be being described inject a frisson of moral danger into love-elegy that seems essential to the effect it seeks.

Also relevant here is the rhetorical character of this poetry. The poet who personally excelled at declamation, and whose verse is primarily directed, we may suspect, at the young men of the Roman elite who enjoyed similar training, is often to be found in the *Amores* indulging the talents we have associated with a star declaimer. The sheer invention required to write wittily to topics such as the similarity of the life of love and the life of the soldier (*Am.* 1.9), the dilemma of being in love simultaneously with two equally desirable women (2.10), the lover's signet ring (2.15), or even his own sexual impotence (3.7), is seeking the same kind of plaudits, favouring power of expression over any practical application, as a declamation sufficiently memorable to be recalled by Seneca the Elder in old age.

An especially outrageous example of Ovid's rhetorical prowess will perhaps reinforce our sense of the moral evasiveness of love-elegy. In both *Amores* 2.19 and 3.4 Ovid addresses a husband, but the arguments in each poem are precisely opposite. In 3.4 his case seems the natural one for a lover to make, that the husband has really nothing to gain by surrounding his wife with security: if she is pure of heart she needs no guard, and various other specious arguments designed to facilitate access. But in 2.19, with comparable persuasive power, the poet had insisted to the contrary that the husband should make a proper effort to protect his wife from characters like himself, because what interest could there possibly be in pursuing a woman if it was made too easy: 'Woe is me, shall I never be prevented from seeing her?', he laments. It perhaps helps to know that 2.19 is the last poem of its book, the book that we recall began with the door being shut in Ovid's face. There in 2.1 we learned that shutting the poet out is what inspires a book of love-elegy. The genius of 2.19 is to end a book with a poem arguing a position that is counterintuitive for a lover, but perfectly explicable for a love poet. For if the poet-lover is not going to be locked out any more, where is a third book of love-elegy going to come from?

Rhetoric and literary play mesh closely here, but whether as crowd-pleasing displays of Ovid's ability to speak *in utramque partem*, on opposed sides of a case with equal plausibility, the Roman rhetorical ideal, or in the case of 2.19 as witty manipulation of genre stereotypes, these two poems may seem highly unlikely to be mistaken for authentic records of immoral behaviour. Nevertheless they play with controversial issues, issues incidentally which in the *Ars Amatoria* are both more explicitly acknowledged and more riskily handled, and which in consequence contribute to the notoriety the latter poem achieved. Something strongly in evidence in 2.19 and 3.4 is the vocabulary of marriage: *uxor*, 'wife', *maritus*, 'husband', and *adulter* which I probably don't need to translate. Generally in the *Amores* Corinna is implied to be a *meretrix*, a courtesan or high-class prostitute, sexual relations with whom, according to standard Roman *mores*, were broadly unobjectionable. Occasionally, though, and certainly in these poems, it seems clear that the poet-lover has adultery with a married woman in view. 3.4 is in fact one place where we can clearly see the influence on love-elegy of the popular theatrical genre of mime: the so-called 'Adultery Mime' featuring lover, wife, and gullible husband is the only mime plot that we can confidently identify. But adultery, as we shall see, was a topic it was perilous to be too flippant about at any stage in Roman history, and particularly in Augustan Rome.

The *Ars Amatoria*, composed between 1 BCE and 2 CE, claims to take Ovid's experience as a lover, gleaned from the escapades recounted in the *Amores* (he more than once professes to 'remember' moments from those poems as illustration of his teaching), and use it to educate his readers in erotic success. The greater detachment this implies, the lover becoming a teacher, might suit an author now into his forties, but the poem is best considered an innovative variation on love-elegy. It isn't quite true to say that Ovid was the last Roman exponent of love-elegy, but he and his readers may well have felt that his *Amores* had exhausted its potential. At any rate, the fundamental inspiration of the *Ars* was again a very literary one, to combine love-elegy with another poetic genre, didactic poetry—poetry that taught its readers, or at least purported to. Didactic poetry traced its history back to the archaic Greek poet Hesiod (an important model for Callimachus), but in Ovid's day it was represented by two especially influential compositions: Lucretius' *De Rerum Natura* ('On the Nature of the Universe'), which explained the world according to the doctrines of the philosopher Epicurus, and Virgil's *Georgics*, on farming. The *Ars Amatoria* teaches men how to find (Book 1) and keep (Book 2) a lover, women how to do the same (Book 3), and then the *Remedia Amoris* explains how to 'unlearn' the lessons of the *Ars*. This might ironically involve rereading the *Ars* (so you know how to find a new love to cure you of the old one): *artes tu perlege nostras*, 'Read our *Arts* thoroughly' he advises the reader of the *Remedia* (487).

Whether or not a didactic poem really aspired to teach the reader (in the case of the *Georgics* this is doubtful, for example), this kind of poetry tackled inherently teachable topics. Thus a possible model for the progress of Ovid's didactic compositions from contagion to cure is provided by the Greek poems of Nicander, the *Theriaka* and *Alexipharmaka* on venomous animals and their antidotes; Ovid's own earlier venture in the form was the *Medicamina Faciei Femineae*, 'Cosmetics for the Female Face', of which unfortunately only a hundred lines survive, but again there was no inherent tension between topic and didactic form. Love, on the other hand, or at least love depicted in love-elegy, is very different from a snake bite, or indeed a recipe for facial make-up. Elegiac love is an irresistible force over which the lover has no control, and the idea it can be reduced to an educational syllabus is inherently ridiculous. *Tu mihi sola places*, 'You're the only one for me!', an impassioned Propertius had assured his lover Cynthia (2.7.19); *elige cui dicas 'Tu mihi sola places'* is the first piece of advice Ovid gives the aspirant lover: 'Select someone to tell "You're the only one for me!"', an exquisite collision of rational choice and passionate impulse. The *Remedia Amoris* summarizes the paradoxical, and uproariously funny, project of the *Ars* when the poet attempts to justify his new venture, making his readers fall *out* of love, to an alarmed love god Cupid: 'Furthermore, I have taught by what skill [*ars*] you could be got, | and what before was *impulse*, is now *rational science*' (9–10). A didactic poem about *amor* thus often comes close to parody. Certainly we find characteristics of the kind of poetry written by Hesiod or Lucretius splendidly misused. Two contradictory tendencies of conventional didactic poetry were to parade its practical, subliterary character and kinship with technical handbooks, and at the same time to identify itself with the very highest form of poetry, epic. At the beginning of the *Ars* Ovid denies he is enjoying any conventional poetic inspiration from Apollo or the Muses: *usus opus mouet hoc*, 'experience alone drives this work' (*AA* 1.29), he mock-pompously insists. The body of the instruction is articulated not as a poem might be, but like a real work of instruction. Here he sets out the contents of the first two books (1.35–8), a systematic course of study incongruously set in the most elegantly turned elegiacs:

> First, work to find an object for your love,
>> you who now for this first time come a soldier to fight new wars.
> The next task is to prevail upon the girl that appeals to you,
>> and the third, to ensure that love lasts a long time.

As for its relationship to epic, such heroes as may find themselves in this poem suffer severe indignities. The first book features the myth of Achilles on Scyros, in which the hero, hidden away and dressed in women's clothes by his mother Thetis to prevent him going to Troy, gives himself away, among other things, by having sex with the princess Deidamia. Ovid's account indulges in extended *double entendre*, Achilles' 'Pelian spear' (in the *Iliad* Achilles' definitive weapon, the only item Patroclus cannot borrow from him) suggesting his genitalia. Such mischievous play with Achilles' epic accoutrements had a long history. Sotades, a scandalous Greek poet of the 3rd century BCE, had recast Homer's description of Achilles' spear so that it described instead Achilles' penis, for the dimensions of which the hero was also traditionally celebrated. When Ovid does smut, you can at least be sure it's smut with a long and prestigious poetic pedigree.

A more immediate point of reference for Ovid is Virgil, both the *Aeneid* and his earlier farming poem *Georgics*. Like the narrator of Virgil's latter poem, Ovid is given to portentous adages. We're told that when Virgil was reciting from the *Georgics* and came to 'Plough undressed and sow undressed' (*Geo.* 1.299, a direct translation of Hesiod), i.e. advice to the farmer that both ploughing and sowing should be done in warm weather, an audience member intruded the metrically perfect supplement 'and you'll get a fever when it's cold'. Ovid's impulse is similar to that ancient heckler. *Hoc opus, hic labor est, primo sine munere iungi*, he asserts, 'This is the task, this the toil, to get lucky without first parting with a present' (1.453), and *hoc opus, hic labor est* is how the Sibyl of Cumae in the *Aeneid* had expressed to Aeneas the difficulty of escaping the Underworld once one had entered it. Ovid rejoices in mock-serious application of rural imagery, reminiscent of the *Georgics*, to love affairs: 'As many hares as feed on Athos, bees on Hybla, | as many berries as the blue-grey tree of Athena bears, | as many shells on the shore, so many are the pains in love' (2.517–19). One such, by the good offices of Erasmus and his influential collection of *Adages*, is still familiar to us: *fertilior seges est alienis semper in agris*, 'The grass is greener over the fence' (*AA* 1.349).

The *Ars* and the *Remedia* may thus seem even more artificial a literary project than the *Amores*, poetry that sought applause for its dexterous fusion of two divergent traditions ahead of anything else. Yet the *Ars Amatoria*, Ovid later insists, was partly responsible for his expulsion from Rome, even though his banishment occurred as many as eight years after the poem was published. The poem could—plausibly, one assumes—condemn him as the *obsceni doctor adulterii*, 'teacher of disgusting adultery' (*Tristia* 2.212), and we need to see how that might be.

If the *Amores* flirted with the possibility that a real lifestyle was being depicted, the *Ars Amatoria* pushes the label further. Most obviously, the Roman context within which the life of love is pursued comes into much sharper focus. When the issue is where to find potential lovers, Ovid identifies monuments or celebrations associated with Augustus, among others: for instance, the portico attached to Augustus' temple of Apollo on the Palatine (1.69–74), the mock naval battle staged by Augustus at the dedication of the Temple of Mars Ultor, marking the revenge he had taken on the assassins of his adoptive father Julius Caesar (1.171–6), and the triumphal procession that Ovid predicts Augustus' grandson Gaius Caesar will soon celebrate over the Parthians (1.177–228). (The temples of Apollo and Mars were highlights of an ambitious building programme that the emperor undertook.) From this latter passage also comes an example of something we identified in the *Amores*, moments of intense familiarity that almost oblige the reader to credit the reality of the scene. As the triumphal procession with its images of obscure locations in the Middle East comes past, the lover is advised to Romansplain: 'And when some girl in the crowd asks the names of kings, | or what places, what mountains, what rivers are being carried along, | answer everything, and do it even if no one asks. | And if you don't know some of them, recite them as if they are entirely familiar to you' (1.219–22). Having only the very vaguest idea what was being paraded in front of you must have been a familiar experience at such public extravaganzas.

But what made all this especially contentious in Augustan Rome was something closely bound up with all the temple construction, the emperor's commitment to the moral rejuvenation of a society only recently emerged from civil conflict—specifically a law he passed in 18 BCE, the *Lex Iulia de adulteriis coercendis*, which for the first time criminalized the act of adultery. Ovid regularly acknowledges in the *Ars* the sharp distinction between *meretrices*, prostitutes, and respectable married women, *matronae*, that this legislation sought to draw, explicitly asserting that his work is strictly for the attention of the former category of women, not the latter. 'How a cunning husband may be deceived, | or a wakeful guard, I was going to pass by. | Let the bride fear her man, let the guarding of a bride be respected: | this is proper, this the laws and right and decency command. | But that *you* be kept under observation, whom the praetor's rod has just recently set free [i.e. *meretrices* who used to be slaves], | who could endure?' (3.611–16). In practice, though, we often feel that we are reading about adultery, not legitimate encounters with prostitutes, and Ovid's insistent claims to the contrary can lack conviction. There will be no criminality in my song, he insists, *inque meo nullum carmine crimen erit* (1.34) but there is a c, r, i, m, e, and n in *carmine*, 'song', according to Latin orthography at least, and Ovid knows perfectly well we'll notice it. The ambiguous status of *meretrices* complicates things further. The orator Cicero was once put out to find himself at a dinner party where one of the other guests was Volumnia Cytheris, a courtesan who was the model for Cornelius Gallus' lover in his elegies, Lycoris. Cicero's discomfort tells us about the traditional attitude to prostitutes in Rome, but Cytheris's presence at a respectable social gathering also indicates the wealth, status, and power which some could in practice attain. Cytheris was over time the mistress of M. Brutus (the assassin of Julius Caesar) and Mark Antony, as well as Gallus. The least one can say is that, where Augustan legislation sought to achieve clarity, Ovid maintains a fuzzy, and no doubt more authentic, picture of sex in the City of Rome, and not one consistently supportive of family values; and this was not, we must assume, the mood music that Augustus sought.

There is much irredeemably Roman, in the sense of deplorable, about Ovid's love poetry. The degraded status claimed for himself by the elegiac lover cannot conceal the fact, for example, that women in this poetry are characterized to a minimal degree, and function in the poetry as stereotypes conforming, in their physical attractiveness, to male sexual fantasies. Even in Book 3 of the *Ars Amatoria*, supposedly advice directed at women, there is a suspicion that the women are being fed guidance that suits the interests of male lovers, and that men remain the primary readership of this book too. The story of Cephalus and Procris, for instance, presented as evidence that one should not suspect your male lover of infidelity too readily (3.687–746), is, given the prominence of versions of the myth where Cephalus *was* unfaithful, a lesson only a naive reader would take at face value. Ovid was also as comfortable as the next Roman with a slave-owning society, and a high tolerance of sexual coercion is on display, for example in the story of Achilles and Deidamia or the Cypassis poems in *Amores* 2, which in particular assume the ready availability of slaves for sexual gratification.

Yet there remains in this poetry, for all that, glimpses of a remarkably independent sensibility. When Ovid defends Helen, in an explicitly adulterous context: *Helenen ego crimine soluo: | usa est humani commoditate uiri*, 'Helen I absolve of guilt: | she availed herself of the opportunity a cultivated man afforded her' (*AA* 2.372); when he insists that male and female sexual partners should enjoy equal pleasure (*AA* 2.681–4); or when he expresses his delight in the present age: 'Let ancient times delight other people: I congratulate myself that I | was not born until now: this age suits my character' (*AA* 3.121–2); this may not seem anything particularly radical from our perspective, but he is contradicting some deeply grounded Roman assumptions, not to mention the ultra-conservative campaign of Augustus.

Ovid himself, in his poetry from exile, reports that the *Ars Amatoria* was banned from public libraries in Rome (*Tristia*

3.1.59–72, one of them adjacent to a portico that Ovid had recommended for erotic assignations), and best kept out of sight even in private collections (*Epistulae ex Ponto* 1.1.12). Censorship of one kind or another is a theme in the later history of Ovid's love poetry, the *Remedia* for obvious reasons generally excepted: to get over a love affair, he advises there (151–4), take up the law, take up soldiering! Christopher Marlowe's line-for-line translations of the *Amores*, published in 1597 but probably composed rather earlier, are at times very successful in capturing the balance and elegance of Ovidian elegiacs in rhymed pentameters, but were banned by the Archbishop of Canterbury John Whitgift in 1599, copies of the poem recalled and publicly burned; at a similar time in Spain, a vernacular commentary on the Song of Songs from the Old Testament by the poet Fray Luis de León was condemned by the Inquisition, and Fray Luis imprisoned, on the basis that it was too much like 'los amores de Ovidio y otros poetas'. Copies of the *Ars Amatoria* were still being barred entry by United States Customs as recently as 1928.

A different form of expurgation was visited upon these notorious texts by the Byzantine monk responsible for preserving selections of Ovid's love poetry in a Greek prose translation. The original translations were probably done by Maximus Planudes, a 13th-century monk and scholar who also turned Ovid's *Heroides* and *Metamorphoses* into Greek. We do not generally expect the Greeks to take much interest in Latin poetry, but Planudes' translation activity was related to a movement to unite the eastern and western Churches, itself associated with the hope that help might be forthcoming from the Christian West to defend Byzantium against the Muslim Turks—not an obvious role for Ovid to play, perhaps. The Greek translations of the *Amores* and *Ars Amatoria* and *Remedia* survive as excerpts in a later collection of texts for educational purposes, and the excerptor, with a view to the young people at whom his anthology was evidently aimed, has an amusing line in bowdlerization. *Amor*, 'love', is rendered as *tode to pragma*, 'this topic', *oscula ferre*, 'kiss', as *proseipein*, 'speak to', *puella*, 'girl', as *philos*, '(male) friend'.

Sometimes, however, our excerptor's concentration lapses, and a case in point is a moment in *Amores* 2.4. In this poem Ovid rues his inability to resist any women in Rome: 'When this woman sings sweetly and fluently modulates her voice, | I wish to snatch kisses as she sings. | This other runs over the mournful strings with nimble thumb: | who could fail to love such skilful hands? | Another appeals to me with her gestures, moving her arms to the rhythm, | and twists her soft body with supple skill: | To say nothing of me, as I am affected by everything, | put Hippolytus in my place and he'll turn into Priapus!' (25–32). Hippolytus was the mythical paradigm of sexual self-restraint, while the god Priapus is best described as a kind of threateningly oversexed scarecrow. But somehow our eagle-eyed Byzantine excerptor fails to censor Priapus, and we have a direct translation of these lines into Greek.

Another medieval engagement with *Am.* 2.4 is more sophisticated, and indeed here Ovid may be credited with inspiring the most celebrated of all medieval Latin lyrics. The *Confession* of the Archpoet, a 12th-century writer, picks up on Ovid's pre-Christian elegiac self-criticism, and the word *confiteor*, 'I confess' (*Am.* 2.4.3) in particular, and reinvents Ovid's poem as a Christian confession to his priestly patron Rainald of Dassel. Hippolytus, though not Priapus, returns in connection with Pavia, an Italian city noted for the pleasures of the flesh; Ovidian elegiacs are now the goliardic metre and rhyme, but a certain Ovidian chutzpah persists: *Si ponas Ypolitum hodie Papie,* | *non erit Ypolitus in sequenti die*, 'Place Hippolytus in Pavia today, | He won't be Hippolytus tomorrow.'

The crucial difference between Ovid's poem and the *Confession* is that the Archpoet gains absolution through his penance, a sacrament unavailable to the pagan Ovid. The *Confession* is thus the most subtle, but also potentially the most devastating, critique of Ovid's love poetry, if by implication it dismisses it as a symptom of pagan ignorance of the Christian revelation.

Hyemf ite superat lacturaf poma miriaf
Super & emedio flamine mella petat
Nihil tibi turpe luuat cure sua cuique voluptas
haec qq abalteriuf grata dolore uenit
heu facimuf noneft hoftif metuenduf amandi
Quof credif fidof effuge tutuf erif
Cognatu fratreque caue caruque fodalem
prebebit ueros haec tibi turba metuf
Finituruf eram fed funt diuerfa puellif
pectora mille animof excipe mille modif
Nec uellus eadem parit omia utabufillif
Conuenit h olerf hic bene farra uirent
pectoribuf moref totfunt quot inorbe figure
Quifapit innumeraf moribuf aptuf erit
Utque leuef proteuf modo fe tenuabit hundaf
Nunc leo nunc arbor nunc erit hirtuf aper
hic iaculo pifcif illic capiuntur abhamif
haec caua contenta retia fune trahunt
Nec tibi conueniat cunctof modus unufadannof
                te
longiuf insidiaf curua uidebit anuf
Sidoceuf indeare rudi petulanf ne pudenti
diffid& mire procanuf illa fibi
Indeft utque fe tunut comtere honufto
Utlif inamplecuf inferioruf erit
Parf fpat cepti parf est exhaufta laborif
hic teneat nraf anchora iacta ratef

3. The last lines of *Ars Amatoria* 1, from 'St Dunstan's Classbook', which may be written in St Dunstan's own hand.

But some balance in this sorry history of suppression is provided by a 9th-century Welsh copy of the *Ars Amatoria* in the Bodleian Library, Oxford, one of the oldest surviving manuscripts of this poem. In the early 10th century it came into the possession of St Dunstan—at one time (before Thomas à Becket) the most popular saint in England. Either because the Welsh original was becoming illegible or because it had been mislaid, the very last leaf of the manuscript (see Figure 3), covering the final twenty-five lines of *Ars Amatoria* 1, appears to be written out in St Dunstan's own hand. That a Christian saint contributed to the survival of this most scandalous poem would certainly have tickled its author.

Chapter 3
Letters of the heroines

In the *Epistulae Heroidum* ('Letters of the Heroines'), strictly speaking two collections of 'single' letters and 'double' letters, the Roman lover of the *Amores* is replaced by a series of mythical women, but they are still complaining about their ill-starred love life. The women of the *Heroides* (as the collection is most commonly known) direct their letters to male lovers who have abandoned them, and since the women and their lovers are in most cases figures from the heroic age, this makes the *Heroides* an important link between the *Amores* and the *Metamorphoses*, Ovid's most ambitious fusion of the erotic and the mythological. To Dryden (far from an uncritical fan of Ovid overall, as we know) these poems 'are generally granted to be the most perfect piece of Ovid'. The concern of much modern scholarship, it's fair to say, has been whether these poems, in part or whole, are by Ovid at all.

The problem of authenticity is worth brief consideration if only because with Ovid it arises quite rarely: the comparative stability of Ovid's texts is one indication that they have maintained a degree of popularity ever since they were written. Ovid's poetry is preserved because it continued to be copied, first for the pagan readers of antiquity and by monks in monastery scriptoria thereafter. Many texts were lost in that process, of course, no copies made and the thread broken—and it need have nothing to do with their intrinsic quality: Ovid's *Medea* is an example of a work highly rated in antiquity that now only exists as three short fragments that happen to have been quoted by other authors. The *Heroides* have survived in full, but seem to have been less popular than Ovid's other works, and thus less copied, at certain moments in the tradition, limiting the witnesses we have to Ovid's original text. Paradoxically, however, the amount of inauthentic material suspected to be present within the *Heroides* collections, up to and including doubts about the authorship of entire poems, also indicates the popularity of this poetic format in antiquity. From the beginning the *Heroides* had imitators: the heroines' letters provoked responses.

In modern editions fifteen love letters addressed by deserted women to their lovers are combined with three exchanges of letters between men and women, Paris and Helen, Leander and Hero, and Acontius and Cydippe. Of the 'single letters', 1–15, there are significant doubts in a number of cases whether they are really Ovid's work, questions of style and quality combining with the evidence of a list provided by Ovid himself (*Am.* 2.18.21–34) to make only *Heroides* 1–2 (Penelope to Ulysses, Phyllis to Demophoon), 4–7 (Phaedra to Hippolytus, Oenone to Paris, Hypsipyle to Jason, Dido to Aeneas), and 10–11 (Ariadne to Theseus, Canace to Macareus) incontestably authentic. But here we enter something of a labyrinth: *Heroides* 3 (Briseis to Achilles) has never been seriously doubted by Ovidian scholars, even though Briseis doesn't feature in Ovid's list in the *Amores*, whereas Sappho *is* included on that list—but *Heroides* 15, the existing letter of Sappho to Phaon, has seemed to most readers simply not accomplished enough to be from Ovid's pen. Tellingly also, *Heroides* 15 comes to us by a manuscript tradition separate from the other poems, only added to the end of the single *Heroides* by the scholar Daniel Heinsius in his edition of 1629. Debate continues, and a case is regularly made for one or other of 8–9, 12–14, and even 15, generally when quality is identified that other scholars have missed, or (say it quietly) when Ovidian authorship is convenient to a particular scholarly argument. Whatever else

40

may be said about *Heroides* 15, specifically, it is a valuable, if typically neglected, source for the perception of Sappho, an archaic Greek poet (not a conventionally mythical figure, unlike the other heroines) who is a rare example of a woman author in antiquity; and the problem of the elusive female voice in Graeco-Roman poetry clings closely to these collections.

The dating of these poems also presents challenges. Whatever we are to imagine that Ovid published as his first book of single letters, he must have done so well before the publication of the second, three-book edition of his *Amores*, which itself preceded the *Ars Amatoria* (and the lost *Medea*). These are some of his earliest poetic compositions, in other words. As for the double letters, 16–21, they may be some of his last. Ovid makes no reference to the double letters elsewhere in his poetry, and certain stylistic and metrical features suggest that they date to his time in exile, after 8 or 9 CE. Doubts about the authenticity of the double letters were once countenanced, but not much any longer, essentially because these poems are far too strong: if they were not by Ovid, 'an *ignotus* has beaten him at his own game', as one scholar (E. K. Rand) has put it. An attractive theory, which also makes sense of the disproportionate length of 16, Paris's letter to Helen, is that *Heroides* 16–21 are an unrevised draft, left unpublished at the poet's death. Whenever the double letters were written, it is worth adding, they represent a conscious continuation and development of the format established in the single letters. But as exile poetry the themes of separation and longing that are key to this poetry would achieve a renewed poignancy.

As texts grounded to an unusual degree in Graeco-Roman culture and taste, the *Heroides* pose a special challenge to anyone seeking to explain their appeal, appealing though they undoubtedly are. But on the principle that a literary text is never more itself than at its end (especially in a literary culture as self-reflexive as Ovid's), one way into this poetry is through *Heroides* 20–1, the letters between Acontius and Cydippe that round off Ovid's experiment in epistolary love poetry. Fortunately these two poems offer self-conscious commentary on the origin of the *Heroides* in the traditions of elegiac poetry, in elite rhetorical training in Rome, and in the ancient art of letter writing; but they manage this meta-literary task, as Ovid is wont to do, within a brilliantly engaging narrative.

The story of Acontius and Cydippe had received its definitive telling in the third book of Callimachus' vastly influential *Aetia*, 'Causes', where it did the antiquarian job of explaining a peculiar marriage custom. Acontius was a young man from the island of Ceos in the Aegean, and had fallen in love with Cydippe, from Naxos, at a festival on the sacred island of Delos. He set out to secure her hand in marriage by a stratagem, throwing in front of her an apple inscribed with the words 'I swear by Artemis to marry Acontius'. Cydippe read the words out loud, at her illiterate nurse's request, and thus unwittingly bound herself by the oath. Repeated attempts by Cydippe's father to marry her off to another young man had to be abandoned when she fell dangerously ill each time the marriage approached. At the fourth attempt Cydippe's father went to Delphi to consult the oracle of Apollo, where the god revealed to him the truth: Acontius and Cydippe were duly married. What Ovid offers is an exchange of letters between the couple at an advanced point in Callimachus' story, Cydippe writing from her sick bed as her father consults the Delphic oracle.

One aspect of *Heroides* 20–1 that both encapsulates and caps off Ovid's experiment in amatory epistolography is the attention they give to the very character of letters. These represented means of communication and organization critical to the functioning of the Graeco-Roman world, one testament to their significance being how extensively discussed and theorized letter writing is in ancient literature and scholarship—another is how successful movements like Christianity could be if they mastered the technology. Letters, as analysed by ancient scholars, are conversations by other means, the ideal letter presenting the writer to the reader as if bodily present: Ovid advises lovers to write letters in such a style *praesens ut uideare loqui* (*AA* 1.468), 'that you seem to be speaking in her presence'. But these advanced skills of composition were only necessary because the letter was by definition an inferior form of communication, something only to be resorted to when authentic, face-to-face conversation was unavailable. Women, whose sequestered lives might favour indirect communication of this kind, became particularly associated with letter writing (and this is not limited to antiquity), and the shortcomings of the epistolary form, as compared with the direct, unmediated communication that was the stereotype of male communication, could thus come to embody the disempowered status of women in a patriarchal society.

Ovid claims his poetic letters as an innovation (*AA* 3.345–6), and despite the partial precedent of a poem by his elegiac predecessor Propertius (4.3), Ovid's book-length realization is indeed an unparalleled achievement. What Propertius' poem and the single *Heroides* have in common, though, is that the letter is a vehicle for the self-expression of a deserted woman, in Propertius' case a wife writing to a husband away at the wars. The very need to write a letter implies disadvantaged circumstances, and the effect is enhanced in Propertius and Ovid's first fifteen poems by their formal isolation: Ovid's 'Letters of the Heroines', as published, receive no answers, and whether the lovers to whom they are addressed even received and read them is left in doubt. This dynamic shifts interestingly in the double letters, where men write first and secure answers to their letters from women, but where there is also scope for the women, writing second, to have the last word argumentatively. Ovid tells us in *Amores* 2.18 that a poet named Sabinus wrote replies to Ovid's heroines from their male lovers, answering an invitation implicit in the poems, and Sabinus' *Epistulae Heroum* is an early reception of Ovid that it would be very good to possess. The role in the process of writing, sending, and reading played by readers like ourselves also needs to be considered, of course. We can share and be persuaded by Ariadne's reproaches of Theseus (*Heroides* 10), or indeed appalled by Canace's incestuous designs on her brother Macareus (*Her.* 11), even if their letters never reached their fictional destination, so there is always 'delivery' of a kind.

Even to the extent that a letter betrays the intrinsic disadvantage of the writer's circumstances, there is scope nevertheless for Ovid to show the tables turned. In *Her.* 18–19 the lovers Hero and Leander, separated both by parental disapproval and the stormy waters of the Hellespont, exchange the most unqualified and touching expressions of affection in Ovid's collection. But the intense desire of the lovers to overcome their separation—there is a comparatively rare piece of overt sensuality in this witty and whimsical poet as Leander anticipates, with transparent metaphor, their lovemaking when they meet (18.205–14)—is haunted by the reader's foreknowledge of their tragic fate. Unable to wait for the storm to abate, Leander will leap into the water, but the light in Hero's window that guides him as he swims will be blown out, causing him to lose his way and drown. In despair Hero will throw herself from her tower. As often in the *Heroides*, Ovid encourages us to wonder where in this tragic tale the exchange of letters falls, and one obvious answer is that it was receiving Hero's letter, a potent mix of anxiety for his safety and yearning to see him, that proved too much for Leander to resist.

If writing sometimes has unusual power to compel (and every letter seeks to impress the wishes of the writer on the recipient to some extent, of course), in Acontius and Cydippe Ovid playfully deploys an ancient pipedream, the missive that brooks no refusal. The 'letter' that secures Cydippe as his wife is inscribed on the apple, or maybe a quince, that Acontius rolls in front of her, but Cydippe's reading of it is cleverly intertwined in Ovid's version with her reading of Acontius' letter. *Perlege*, Acontius insists at the start of his letter, 'Read to the end!' (20.3), but we only really understand the intensity of Cydippe's reluctance to do so when we hear that *perlege* was exactly what her nurse had asked her to do with the words on the apple (21.109).

Acontius and Cydippe is thus a story all about letters and the power of writing, featuring the ultimate in epistolary communication. The other 'Letters of the Heroines' often require considerable ingenuity on Ovid's part to locate the act of letter writing plausibly within a pre-existing mythical storyline. Ovid, being Ovid, is not averse at times to exposing the *implausibility* of the scenario: it is hard to see how Ariadne's letter will get away from the island on which she has been abandoned if she can't, but also how such an emotionally frenzied reaction to Theseus' betrayal could translate itself into the disciplined exercise of letter composition. Briseis opens her letter to Achilles (*Her.* 3.1–4) by apologizing for her poor Greek and for the smudging of her words caused by her tears, but of course we read her Latin verse on a clean page, acutely aware at that moment of the artificiality of Ovid's project. (Canace warns that her letter may be stained with blood, as she sits with pen in right hand and dagger in left in case her brother fails to acquiesce.) But at other moments the fit is all but seamless, as it is in Penelope's letter to Ulysses, the opening poem of the collection. Here regular reminders of the plot of Homer's *Odyssey*, combined with the information Penelope provides that she hands a letter for Ulysses to any stranger that visits (1.59–62), allow us to conclude that the visitor to whom she will give *this* letter will be none other than Ulysses himself, by this stage of the *Odyssey* restored to Ithaca in disguise. Don't bother writing back to me, Penelope tells her husband at the start of her letter, but *ipse ueni* (1.2), 'come in person', making this an unusually efficacious missive at the beginning to match Acontius' at the end.

Penelope in *Her.* 1 and Briseis in *Her.* 3, characters 'borrowed' by Ovid from pre-existing literature, represent a central strategy of the *Heroides*, to open new windows in familiar texts, and here

Ovid's irrepressible interest in genre has a role to play. These poems are self-consciously elegiac in character as well as in metrical form, figures from the heroic realm recast as lovers, and the condition of the heroines who write the letters consistently recalls the lovers of love-elegy, their unanswered prayers and insurmountable separation from the loved one so reminiscent of the *exclusus amator*. (The older association of elegiacs with lament is also regularly felt.) The very title of this collection embodies an agenda, 'Heroines' a provocative twist on a more conventional presence in poetry, the masculine heroes of epic: 'Letters of the She-heroes' might better capture its scandalous force. Genre is unavoidably gendered in Roman poetry, and women's self-expression in elegiac couplets is in both respects at creative variance with the normative poetic form of epic: manly men called Achilles or Aeneas in a vehicle known as 'heroic verse'. Penelope's letter is typical of the single *Heroides* in that it features as author-protagonist a woman from pre-existing heroic literature, but a woman who, in this new elegiac environment, can voice a markedly different perspective. Similarly Dido, queen of Carthage, already a troublingly elegiac presence in Virgil's epic *Aeneid*, a lover rejected by the hero and the poem as he pursues his destiny to found Rome, is in *Her.* 7 given free rein to express her dissenting sensibility. Briseis is a marginal character in Homer's *Iliad* allowed here to share her view of Achilles' role, and best interests, in the Trojan War, while Oenone in *Her.* 5, the nymph who was Paris's lover before he left to find Helen, introduces more generic complexity, a pastoral figure as well as elegiac lover. But over Oenone's story also looms the violent plot of the *Iliad* that Paris's elopement with Helen will trigger, so here too the perpetual tussle between the values of elegy and epic is in play.

But can Briseis really be considered 'marginal' to the plot of the *Iliad*? She does not feature very prominently as a character, it is true, but it is she who motivates Achilles' withdrawal from the Achaean camp, when taken from Achilles by Agamemnon to

Ovid

replace his captive Chryseis, and thus in a sense Briseis drives the entire plot of Homer's poem. The familiarity of these characters to Ovid's readers generates many rich ironies, as their own understanding of their circumstances confronts what we know about them: Penelope is not the only one whose letter seems to arise quite organically from a pre-existing telling of the story, and thus to endorse the narrative of Homer or Virgil from which the heroine has come. But there is a more radical way of understanding the relationship that is established between traditional and Ovidian accounts, a reading against the grain of the tradition which might pose the question why the masculine priorities of one poem should trump the feminine of another. Ovid is offering us an elegiac reading of the mythical past to compete with epic. Whose perspective on pitiless warfare has more weight, once we have read Briseis's compelling account in *Heroides* 3, Homer's or her own?

What is again somewhat untypical about Acontius and Cydippe, and yet true in another sense to the role of these poems as capstones to the larger collection, is that they originate, not in an epic poem, but in Callimachus, and in his greatest poem. Theirs was in fact the most popular story in the most popular poem of this most popular poet in Hellenistic Greece. In my opening chapter I quoted Ovid in the *Remedia Amoris* describing the proper application of the epic hexameter and elegiacs in a way that implies that Cydippe could stand for Callimachus' entire poetic achievement. In Ovid's poems, as she wastes away from the sickness sent by the goddess, she begins to suggest the 'skinny Muse' (i.e. polished poetry lacking any excess) that Callimachus had presented as an ideal in the prologue to the *Aetia* (an important source of poetic imagery for Roman poets). There is thus something archetypally elegiac about *Heroides* 20–1 as well as intrinsically epistolary: hints that their story featured in Cornelius Gallus' love-elegy even associate Acontius and Cydippe with the origins of Rome's favourite permutation of elegiac verse.

One effect of having a figure of myth compose a letter is to translate her into a contemporary world. Dryden commented that Ovid 'perhaps has Romaniz'd his *Grecian* Dames too much, and made them speak sometimes as if they had been born in the City of *Rome*, and under the Empire of *Augustus*'. Elegy after love-elegy, in a similar way to letter writing, suggests the conditions of Ovid's Rome, and indeed Paris and Helen flirt over a Mycenean dinner table as contemporary Roman lovers do in *Amores* 1.4, or are instructed to do at *Ars Amatoria* 1.569–84. 'Paris and Helen are masks for fashionable Roman intriguers,' writes one scholar (E. J. Kenney), 'and the legendary setting a vehicle for an entirely modern display of wit, elegance, and flippancy.' But another thing the women authors of these letters take on is the love-elegist's self-awareness. As authors committing their passions to (versified) writing, they resemble poets. There is an intensely evocative moment in *Her.* 19, Hero to Leander, where the heroine refers to her own writing (151–4):

Look! The lamp has sputtered—I am writing with it beside me—
    it has sputtered and given us a favourable omen.
There, nurse is dripping wine onto the auspicious flames,
    and says 'Tomorrow there shall be more of us,' and takes a swig
        herself.

The bibulous nurse is a stock comic character of long standing. Here, though, she gives voice to something fraught with irony, her word for 'more', *plures*, equally interpretable as 'the majority', 'the dead'. 'Tomorrow we shall be dead,' the nurse unwittingly predicts, as she interferes with a lamp that *we* are anxiously aware will cause Leander's death once it is extinguished. Alongside all of this, Hero's writing of her letter by the lamp conforms to a Hellenistic ideal of the poet, polishing her writing through the night by lamplight. There are disturbing implications here for the power of poetry, its capacity to motivate the tragic events that this tableau anticipates.

One further contributory element of fundamental importance to the *Heroides*, once again brought to the fore in the last two poems, returns us to the legal training pursued by the youthful Ovid. What Acontius and Cydippe's exchange of letters has, in addition to everything else, is a tangibly legalistic quality. Acontius presents himself as a lover reinforced by the very best legal advice: 'Love was the learned Counsel that made me cunning in the law,' he informs Cydippe (*Her.* 20.30). Unfortunately for Acontius, he encounters in his future wife someone quite as legally astute as he is, and in *her* letter she triumphantly refutes his claims by a principle familiar to lawyers in antiquity, the distinction between the letter and the spirit. Cydippe read out the oath to marry Acontius, for sure, but that does not mean she swore to marry him. This unexpected realization of Cydippe as a resourceful adversary for Acontius is much of Ovid's aim here: neither figure had been much developed in Callimachus' version of the story, and the letters between them, as with the rest of the *Heroides*, are tours de force of characterization. In this mythical context, in any case, the legalities are neither here nor there, and the goddess Artemis/Diana insists on a marriage. The *Heroides* thus end most satisfactorily on an intellectual victory for a woman, but a mutually agreeable marriage nonetheless.

Law is inseparable from rhetorical training, the declamation (with a view to practising the law) in which the young Ovid, notwithstanding his idiosyncrasies, had excelled. The kinship of the *Heroides*, letters with much of the character of spoken monologues (we recall that Ovid mentions pantomimes or balletic performances that were made of some of his poetry, most likely the *Heroides*), with the declamatory exercises of trainee lawyers has long been noted. In the past the influence of declamation on Ovid's letters has been overstated, and more recently the implication resisted that he has just written rhetorical exercises in verse. But as with the *Amores*, Ovid was himself an aficionado of creative rhetoric, and that goes also for much of his Roman readership. It may not make it easier for us to appreciate this poetry, but the sheer rhetorical inventiveness of these characters, finding the material to talk engagingly to their circumstances for 200 lines, is not the least pleasure that Ovid's contemporaries would have got from them.

Thus Leander's ability in *Her.* 18 to weave complaints out of night swimming, the indulgence he hopes for from the moon (given her love for Endymion) and the stormy north wind (lover of Orithyia), is its own reward, even as we catch a hint of absurdity at the circumstances: the odd mix of amusement and pathos, typical of the *Heroides*, is never more marked than in the letters between these two doomed lovers. Phyllis, abandoned by Theseus' son Demophoon in *Her.* 2, gets splendid mileage from her lover's comparative anonymity in the mythical tradition: under Theseus' statue in Athens will be recorded Sciron, Procrustes, Sinis, the Minotaur, Thebes, the Centaurs, and the Underworld, the full litany of Theseus' heroic exploits, but under Demophoon's just a single pentameter, *hic est cuius amans hospita capta dolo est*, 'This is the man who tricked his loving host' (2.74). Hypsipyle argues herself, out of jealousy for Jason's new lover Medea, into a duplicate of her notoriously bloodthirsty rival: she would be 'a Medea to Medea' (6.151) if she ever encountered her. Penelope delivers a superb declamatory paradox when posing the question to her wandering husband what benefit *she* has gained from the Greeks' successful sack of Troy. Nothing has changed for her: *diruta sunt aliis, uni mihi Pergama restant*, 'For others has Troy been destroyed, for me alone it still persists' (*Her.* 1.51). Then the witty twist (66–8): better if Troy *was* still standing—at least I'd know where you were!

Law, letters, and Hellenistic literature offer some clues to the contemporary appeal of the *Heroides*, then. In some of the most recent scholarship the attention has been on the women protagonists, and the extent to which a feminine perspective, so desperately lacking in Graeco-Roman literature, might be recovered from these poems, the most ambitious and extended presentation of women's experience in Roman literature. Can an author as dead as Ovid liberate his creations to speak a woman's truth? The approach has refreshed scholarship on the poems, but what is hard to deny is how appealing the image of women's desires that Ovid serves up is to a fairly conventional male sensibility in Rome. Cydippe's description of her own sickly body may remind us of Callimachus' Muse, but in its passive availability it also answers to certain male fantasies that Acontius is not alone in enjoying. Ovid's willingness to expose his fiction to view in its own way underlines the true nature of this collection, the purported words of distressed heroines as ventriloquized by a male poet with some authentically Roman attitudes to relations with the opposite sex.

In a sense that has always been the debate with the *Heroides*. The reputation of these poems has ebbed and flowed more dramatically than most of Ovid's poetry, until quite recently also sidelined in scholarship. Unusually, they enjoyed an intense popularity, outstripping all Ovid's other poems, for a quite circumscribed period of time in the long 18th century. This wasn't an entirely isolated moment of celebrity. Chaucer's Man of Law compares his creator's *Legend of Good Women* to its most important model, the *Heroides*: 'For he hath toold of loveris up and doun | Mo than Ovide made of mencioun | In his Episteles, that been ful olde' (53–5). Chaucer's more recent model in the latter work, Giovanni Boccaccio and his *De Claris Mulieribus*, 'On Famous Women', made similarly free use of the *Heroides*. But the reasons for their particular vogue with Dryden and his contemporaries is the comparatively sincere expression of love they were felt to contain (as we move toward the Romantics), while also satisfying an (English) Augustan taste for rhetoric. The combination is exemplified in Alexander Pope's *Eloisa to Abelard* (1717), the 12th-century Latin letters of Heloise to her former lover converted into a Heroic epistle deeply indebted to his Roman precursor.

But the *Heroides* could also provide a model for female self-expression that carried with it the heft and authority of classical antiquity. Thus Marie-Jeanne L'Héritier, in a celebration of the poet Antoinette Deshoulières, *Le Parnasse reconnoissant, ou le triomphe de Madame Des-houlières* (1694), could claim Ovid, on the basis of the *Heroides*, as an ally in the struggle for women's equality. Similarly Lady Mary Wortley Montagu, Pope's unrequited affection for whom informs *Eloisa to Abelard*, exploits the Ovidian model in *Epistle from Mrs Y[onge] to her Husband* to deplore the sexual double standards from which married women suffered, and the power of the platform that Ovid lent Mrs Yonge is undoubted. In more subtle ways, too, the renewed popularity of the *Heroides* coincided in England with increased female literacy, and changes in the perception as well as the experience of women, a greater willingness to see men as the more sexually uninhibited gender, for example, which tended in turn to favour a construction of women as innocent victims, and make the naive country nymph Oenone in *Her.* 5 the most admired of the heroines.

Ovid's contribution to female self-expression is beyond doubt, then, but refreshing all the same is the broadside delivered *To Ovid's Heroines in his Epistles* (1688) by Jane Barker, bluntly rejecting the ideal of female passivity she saw in Ovid's poems, and proposing a more aggressive response to their abandonment:

> Bright *Shees*, what Glories had your Names acquir'd
> Had you consum'd those whom your Beauties fir'd,
> Had laugh'd to see them burn, and so retir'd.

Chapter 4
Metamorphoses

The *Metamorphoses*, Ovid's poem of change, has from the beginning had the status of the poet's masterpiece: in the first book of his exile poetry (*Tristia* 1.7.11–14) Ovid offers it as a better portrait of himself than a sculpted image. Its composition, together with the first six books of the *Fasti*, occupied the second half of his fifth decade, or what turned out to be his last years in Rome. More helpfully for its interpretation, the *Met.* is an epic, conventionally the most ambitious undertaking available to a poet, and in its size (fifteen books when Virgil's *Aeneid* had just twelve), form (dactylic hexameters, the heroic metre, a departure from the elegiacs of Ovid's other poetry), and sweep (Ovid's narrative encompasses the whole of history, and the entire physical world), the poem blazons that higher ambition.

But what ensured the lasting impact of this poem is something else. It is in the *Met.* that we encounter Icarus flying too close to the sun, King Midas' golden touch, Pyramus and Thisbe communicating through a crack in the wall, Diana angrily transforming Actaeon into a deer, Pygmalion's statue coming alive, and Narcissus falling in love with his own reflection. Whether in the Middle Ages, under the title of *Ovidius Maior*, 'the Greater Ovid', or as the 'Bible' of visual artists from the Renaissance onwards, or in collections for modern children like Enid Blyton's *Tales of Ancient Greece* (1930), the *Met.* has served as the authoritative encyclopedia of Graeco-Roman folklore. As we shall see, Ovid would be surprised to find himself the definitive version of anything.

The freshness and vibrancy of Ovid's storytelling has a lot to do with the approach he adopts to writing an epic, a profoundly irreverent one. Ovid, according to Quintilian (a Roman educator writing about a century later), was 'mischievous even in epic', *lasciuus in herois quoque* (10.1.89). Epic, Quintilian implies, is a fundamentally serious business. But the *Met.* is a poem that sets out to amuse: a humble fisherman (in fact the girl Mestra momentarily transformed into the shape of one) is addressed not as a fisherman but 'O ye that conceal the dangling | bronze with a little food, you governor of the rod' (8.855–6); Io is afraid to speak, once restored from bovine to human form (as the Egyptian goddess Isis), in case she emits a moo (1.745–6); Daedalus designs the labyrinth with such cunning that 'scarcely could he himself find the entrance again' (8.167–8). As such the *Met.* is deliberately abusing the dignity, in language and subject matter, that the epic genre demands. We should not be told, when the hero Perseus first sets eyes on the beautiful Andromeda, manacled to a rock above the sea, that he almost forgot to flap his wings (4.677), but it illustrates how an appropriately impressive epic narrative can be punctured by an incongruous flash of wit, Ovid's trademark *ingenium*. Comparable, though darker (and the variation in tone is typical of this poem), is the death of Orpheus. The bard, whose music was famously able to enchant inanimate objects, is unable to charm away the stones hurled at him by Bacchanals because their cries and raucous music drown out the sound of his lyre (11.15–18). In the Io story Jupiter, king of the Gods, and embodiment of the authority claimed by epic poetry (the narratives of both the *Iliad* and the *Aeneid* claim some kind of identity with Jupiter's will, and we recall his abortive appearance in *Amores* 2.1), becomes a comic figure when Juno begins to suspect his liaison with Io. He is obliged, after hiding Io under a cloud, and then under the semblance of a cow, to present her to his wife as a gift: 'What was he to do? It is cruel to hand over his beloved, | suspicious not to' (1.617–18).

I have suggested that the poet who boasted of being to elegy what Virgil was to epic never truly gave up being an elegist, even when writing hexameter poetry. Sufficient evidence of this we have already seen (Quintilian's is a succinct formulation), but what it also entails is that the *Met.* is an epic intensely aware of, and sceptical of, its epic status. If Ovid breaks the unwritten rules of the form, and he does so constantly, he also ensures that his reader is alert to the conventions that he is flouting. When Actaeon stumbles into the clearing where the goddess Diana and her nymph companions are bathing, he sees the goddess's nakedness, and suffers the punishment of being devoured in deer form by his own dogs, because Diana is taller than all the nymphs that try to shield her from view (3.181–2)—a truly mischievous detail. But the superlative height of Diana/Artemis had long been a motif of serious epic poetry, a point of comparison for the stately beauty of the princess Nausicaa in Homer's *Odyssey* and Queen Dido in the *Aeneid*. There is a respectful way of handling these higher beings, we are reminded, but it is not Ovid's way.

Often, since one sign of epic's solemnity is its distance from ordinary life, this can feel like a greater realism, especially when allied to elegy's interest in emotion and psychology: when the gods Jupiter and Mercury, in human disguise, visit two old peasants, Baucis and Philemon, there is a wonderfully vivid scene as the couple's guard-goose eludes the aged couple when they try to catch and butcher it for their divine guests, and runs to the gods for mercy (8.684–8). A talent for realizing in imaginable terms an intrinsically fabulous circumstance is just as clear in the chariot of the sun bearing Phaethon, careering out of control through the star signs (2.169–200), and in Ovid's characterization of the god *Somnus*, 'Sleep', visited by the messenger goddess Iris, who can scarcely rouse himself to listen to her, 'sinking back again and again | and striking his chest with his nodding chin' (11.619-20), falling back into slumber the moment he has done her bidding.

Elegy can make its presence more immediately felt, both in the kinds of story that Ovid favours and the way he tells those stories. There is a gorgeous example of Ovid's sophisticated reworking of his own writing at the end of his treatment of Orpheus, which, including Orpheus' own adventures and the stories that this mythical storyteller sings, extends from the start of Book 10 all the way into Book 11, 800 lines in total. There finally in Book 11, stoned to death by Thracian Bacchanals, he rejoins his wife Eurydice in the Underworld—at the start of Book 10 his failure to rescue his dead wife from the Underworld had been described, the singer unable to resist looking back at her (the rule the gods of the Underworld had imposed upon him) as he walked ahead toward the Upper World. But when Orpheus joins her in death that is all forgotten: 'Here they stroll together, side by side, | or else now Orpheus follows as she goes first, or walks ahead | and looks back, as he now safely can, at his Eurydice' (11.64-6). The allusion is to the mistake that once lost him Eurydice, but also recalls—and enriches beautifully with the extra freight of Orpheus' story—a scene in the *Ars Amatoria* depicting the first stages of a relationship: 'Or if the spacious Colonnade be trodden by her with feet at leisure, | join her there yourself and share her free time; | try now to walk in front of her, now to follow from behind, | now to hurry, now go slowly' (*AA* 1.493-6). Orpheus and Eurydice are young lovers again, not even married yet (the condition of the elegiac lovers in the *Amores* and *Ars Amatoria*): it is as if the whole of Book 10 hadn't happened.

When Perseus is too smitten to remember to flap his wings, or Diana too stately to be effectively screened, one thing that happens is that we are made forcefully aware of the poet's involvement in his poem, the creative intelligence manipulating our responses. This, the greater visibility of the poet, is another

Callimachean, thus elegiac, characteristic of the *Met.*, and it finds explicit expression at the opening and end of the poem. The brisk prologue (1.1–4) promises an account of 'shapes changed into strange bodies' from the very creation of the world *ad mea tempora*, 'up to my times'; while for epilogue, as we saw in the opening chapter, Ovid delivers a ringing celebration of his personal achievement. When he later tried to use the *Met.* from exile to argue his loyalty to the emperor, he quoted his own prologue, but adapted *ad mea tempora* to *in tua tempora, Caesar*, 'up to *your* times, Caesar' (*Tristia* 2.560). The charge here is thus both generic, a puncturing of epic objectivity, and political. The politics of the *Met.* have been endlessly debated, Ovid's treatment of Augustus on his rare appearances in the poem closely analysed. But it is the marginalization of the emperor and the concomitant prominence of the poetic *ego* that may be most telling.

Implied in all of this is the poem's acute self-awareness, a remarkable feat of narrative, encompassing scores of separate stories, which consistently betrays itself *as* a fictional narrative, not least in its intense interest in the creation of art. That might be Arachne weaving a tapestry highly suggestive of Ovid's own texture of love, metamorphosis, and divine misdemeanours, and turned into a spider by her rival Minerva, goddess of handicrafts (6.1–145: an ironic note of self-condemnation from the poet); or Byblis writing and rewriting the letter confessing her love for her own brother (9.517–67)—this evocation of the tortured process of composition and deletion exposes to view the true nature of writing, the labour and imperfection that underlies its final form in Ovid's polished verse. At some level here we are apprehending Byblis as an embodiment of the book, Greek *bublos* or *biblos* (cf. 'Bible').

A text so adept at making plausible characters of incorporeal phenomena like Sleep is thus also keen to reveal (and revel in) its own workings. A representative moment concerns Boreas, the North Wind, enamoured of Orithyia, an Athenian princess

(6.675–721). To begin with, Ovid explains, the wind set about courting the girl in conventional fashion, but to no avail. Disappointed, Boreas takes himself to task. What was a wind doing using blandishments and persuasion? 'Force suits me; by force I drive the gloomy clouds, | with force I twist the seas and overturn the gnarly oaks, | and harden the snows and beat the lands with hail!' (6.690–2). Down he then swoops, and carries Orithyia off forcibly to his chilly northern home. The Latin word for 'force' here is *uis*, and Ovid is playing with ancient analyses of the Latin word for 'wind', *uentus*, which traced it back to *uis*, thereby also (according to the theory of such etymologizing) identifying an essential characteristic of the thing so named: *uis* was of the essence of *uentus*. This is what Ovid's North Wind is newly realizing about himself: he is by definition violent, we might say, and the result is a marvellous collision of mytho-poetic and 'scientific' perceptions of the world. Such different modes of explanation of the physical world are also found coexisting in respectable epics like Virgil's *Aeneid*, where there is play on the ambiguous status of Atlas, for instance, both living giant and mountain of solid rock. But here in the *Met.* the contradictions are brought to the surface and exploited for comic effect in the blustering wind's anguished self-analysis. (The model of interaction between male and female from which Ovid constructs this episode we shall consider later.)

Our ultimate destination here is the theme that, if anything manages the task, binds this poem together, metamorphosis. The *Met.* claims to be a collection of stories about change, and although often we find ourselves hunting around for the metamorphosis in any given story, the transformation of humans into animals, birds, rock, trees, flowers, streams, and much, much more is the common factor in them all. Often the shapes newly assumed by characters have an aptness to their pre-existing character, the superlative weaver Arachne transformed by Minerva into the spider, for example, and the inhabitants of the island of Pithecusae, punished by Jupiter for their dishonesty, turned from men into ugly sub-humans—the monkeys (Greek *pithekos*) from which Pithecusae derived its name (14.90–100).

A more subtle example comes in the course of a convoluted account of the creation of the crow and the re-coloration of the raven from white to black, an episode indebted to Callimachus' poem *Hecale*. The crow explains how, when still a mortal woman, she had been chased by the god Neptune *cum per litora lentis | passibus, ut soleo, summa spatiarer harena*, 'When, as is my habit, I was pacing over the beach with leisurely steps, on the surface of the sand' (2.572–3). Ovid here connects the character pre- and post-metamorphosis by recalling a moment in Virgil's *Georgics* where a crow is described (*Geo.* 1.389): *et sola in sicca secum spatiatur harena*, 'and paces alone and by itself on the dry sand', the crow's high-stepping manner beautifully captured. It is a typically sophisticated moment in Ovid's text, a human's behaviour foreshadowing the essence of themselves that will be their metamorphosed shape (her 'as is my habit', *ut soleo*, betrays an awareness of the continuity on the crow's part, in fact). But Ovid here also draws out the affinity that the process of shape-shifting bears to the very act of literary composition. Metamorphosis in this instance is close to metaphor, the allusion to Virgil implying that the girl was already 'like a crow' and her transformation a kind of metaphor made flesh. Bound up in this fascinating literary game is allusion itself, a key technique of classical literature, the creation of (new) meaning from pre-existing poetry.

Sometimes the issue seems to be how meaning is made. When Perseus, armed with the severed head of Medusa, punishes Atlas for his lack of hospitality by turning him to stone, Atlas becomes Mt Atlas (4.657). Ovid's Latin, *mons factus Atlas*, can be construed in two separate ways that capture Atlas' state before and after his metamorphosis: 'Atlas became a mountain' and 'he became Mt Atlas', the meaning of the expression mutating as Atlas endures his transformation from man to mountain. The disorientation we experience here is very much part of Ovid's plan.

The story of the raven and the crow is a superbly—and quite deliberately—discombobulating episode that not only brings together two species of birdlife that the Roman evidently found it as hard to distinguish as we do, but also compounds our confusion with a cast of human characters whose names, Coronis, Coroneus, and Corone, all suggest the Greek word for crow, *korone*. It is pleasing that when Chaucer in *The Manciple's Tale* retells Ovid's story of Coronis, and the betrayal of her infidelity by the *raven* to her lover Phoebus Apollo, he falls straight into Ovid's trap by misidentifying the relevant corvid as a *crow*.

A similar impulse draws the narrative repeatedly toward paradoxical, conceptually unstable circumstances: the pursuit of the uncatchable fox by the unstoppable dog in Book 7, or the figure *Inuidia*, Envy, who 'gnaws and is gnawed all at once, | and is her own punishment' (*carpitque et carpitur una | suppliciumque suum est*, 2.781–2), Ovid managing there to be both contradictory and psychologically acute. Althaea is pious in her impiety (8.477) as she brings about her son Meleager's death for slaying her brothers; similarly Procne as she cooks her son Itys out of revenge on her husband Tereus for his rape of her sister Philomela. Earlier, when Tereus sets eyes on his sister-in-law, 'whenever she embraced her father | he would wish to be her father (and be no less impious that way!)' (6.481–2). Speeches by Myrrha as she contemplates sex with her father, Byblis with her brother, or Scylla with her father's mortal enemy, allow the delight in memorable paradox so beloved of contemporary declamatory culture, but also have us reflecting on semantic instabilities that admirably suit the poem's theme. 'You see how many laws and names you confound,' Myrrha berates herself: 'Will you be your mother's rival and your father's mistress? | Will you be called the sister of your son and mother of your brother?' (10.346–8). Metamorphosis and paradox are especially closely intertwined when Mestra, gifted the power to take any shape by Neptune, is delighted *a se | se quaeri*, 'to be asked herself | about herself'

(8.862–3), when her master enquires of her, in her new form as a fisherman, whether she has seen anyone like herself.

The metamorphic character of the *Met.* is thus not restricted to explicit descriptions of shape-shifting. In a more profound sense Ovid's epic is devoted to destabilizing the order and certainties that conventional epic was designed to uphold, and metamorphosis is well adapted to advance that end. Nothing in the *Met.* seems predictable, beginning with the plot itself. Unified, theoretically at least, by the theme of change, Ovid's poem is actually a series of short tales, or tales within tales, linked together in ways that often highlight a fundamental lack of connection between them. A favourite conceit, for example, is a transition between stories achieved by someone or something uniquely *unrelated* to what has preceded. In Book 6 the slaughter of Niobe's children at Thebes by Apollo and Diana, avenging Niobe's claim of superiority over *their* mother Latona, segues into the tale of Tereus and Philomela by means of the singular *failure* of Philomela's city Athens, out of all the neighbouring cities, to convey its sympathy to the Thebans. How one story mutates into another is another kind of inexplicable transformation.

Equally capricious is the tone of the poem, wildly divergent within, let alone between, different stories. Hercules, dying in agony from the poisoned shirt of Nessus, violently seizes hold of Lichas, the servant who had innocently brought it to him, and hurls him into the sea. But after the horror of Hercules' protracted and excruciating death, the process of the poison eating away at his flesh presented in grisly detail, the flight and transformation of Lichas is a beautifully extended word picture: 'he, soaring through the airy breezes, hardened into stone, | and as they say rain is frozen by chill winds, | hence snow comes about, and the soft substance of whirling snow, | too, is packed and into solid hail stones, | so he, hurled through the emptiness by the strong arms of Hercules, | fear draining his blood and losing all moisture, | was turned into hard flint, an older age has told' (9.219–25). Episodes of near-tragic intensity like the relentless slaughter of each of Niobe's seven sons and seven daughters by Apollo and Diana (6.204–312), or of extreme violence such as Apollo's flaying of Marsyas (6.382–400), sit alongside the Lycian peasants whose croaking when turned into frogs is audible in Ovid's Latin: *quamuis sint sub aqua, sub aqua maledicere temptant*, 'although they were under water, under water they tried to speak ill' (6.376). A secure moral standpoint to assess these events is denied us, and an aesthetic detachment characterizes even the most disturbing moments: *quid me mihi detrahis*, Marsyas asks Apollo: 'Why do you tear me from myself?' Marsyas is declaiming at the god even as he is being flayed alive.

There is manipulation of readers' expectations here, and an underlying 'metamorphic' sensibility, but a familiar formal issue, too. We have seen in relation to the *Amores*, and will see again in the *Fasti*, that the matter of the continuity or discontinuity of a poetic text was a battleground in the literary polemics that Roman literature had adopted and adapted from Hellenistic Greece. In the preface to the *Met.* Ovid defines the poem to come (especially in the formulation *perpetuum deducite . . . carmen*, 'spin the unbroken song') in terms that a reader familiar with the most influential of the Hellenistic poets, Callimachus, would recognize to be pulling in two directions simultaneously, promising both an extended epic and a poem displaying the meticulous technique that Callimachus promoted. In other words—and how very typical of Ovid this is—the *Met.* is billing itself *both* as the stereotypical epic, an uninterrupted account of great deeds, *and* as its precise opposite, a Callimachean-elegiac collection of short, loosely related compositions. At a moment like the transition between Philomela and Niobe we see this contradictory programme realized: continuity between stories is indeed achieved, but in ways that simply underline how spurious the continuity really is.

Book divisions, as places where even conventional epics pause, provide Ovid with some predictable fun. Book 2 ends with

4. **Europa, and Jupiter as a beautiful (and knowing) bull, House of Jason, Pompeii.**

Jupiter's designs upon Europa (Figure 4), daughter of the king of Tyre, in pursuit of whom the god turns himself into a beautiful bull: 'his colour was of snow that the prints of rough | feet have not trampled nor the watery South Wind melted. | His neck bulged with muscles, a dewlap hung from his fore-quarters, | and his horns, though small, were such as you could maintain | were made by hand, more translucent than a flawless gem' (2.852–6). Europa is tempted to climb upon the bull's back, and it is thus, clutching one of Jupiter's horns as he edges ever closer to the sea, that the book ends, the story incomplete.

One thing that Ovid is doing here is beating epic at its own game, allowing the narrative to flow even from book to book: compared with the books of Virgil's *Aeneid*, which tend to be quite self-contained, this is indeed 'an unbroken song', spectacularly so, barely pausing to drawing breath between 1.1 and 15.879. But given Jupiter's designs on Europa, and making some generalizing but not unreasonable assumptions about Ovid's core Roman readership, the interruption of this narrative is likely to have caused them some fustration. Europa's loose clothes fluttering in the breeze (recalling an image familiar to Ovid's readers from domestic wall paintings), not to mention the erotic image of the horn, anticipate the sexual encounter that will follow Europa's abduction. But turning to Book 3, we discover that this encounter has been entirely elided, and the story moves smartly on to the search by Cadmus for his sister Europa, the upshot of which is Cadmus' foundation of the city of Thebes. The frustration would be greater for an ancient reader, since their text of the poem would be fifteen separate book rolls, *uolumina* (see Figure 5). In other words, that titillated Roman reader is not just turning a modern page, but throwing aside one volume and searching out Volume 3, a much less convenient operation.

Ovid's wit is too rich to be limited to a single effect, however. Another application of the word for horn, *cornu*, it has been pointed out, is the bosses at either end of the sticks around which the book roll was wound: 'unrolled right to its horns' is how the epigrammatist Martial, a century later, describes an apparently fully read book (11.107.1–2). We encounter Jupiter's horns when we reach the horns of the volume, in other words, and are *very* aware of the book we are reading as we finish it. Needless to say, once an expectation of a narrative uninterrupted even by bookends is established, it becomes disruptive to round off a book in unexpectedly conventional fashion. Book 9 closes with the delightful story of Iphis and Ianthe, its conclusion, Iphis's metamorphosis from woman to man (which allows Iphis and Ianthe to be married), profoundly satisfying just when that has become the very last thing that the reader of the *Met.* expects.

The pause between *Met.* 2 and 3 points to another aspect of the *Met.*, and Europa's name is a strong clue. A princess of Tyre in modern Lebanon, Jupiter carries her to Crete, where she bestows her name on the new continent. The space between the books is

5. An image from the Casa del Cenacolo in Pompeii of a young man, perhaps a poet, holding a *uolumen* or book roll: a label (in Latin, *index*) identifies the author of the text on the scroll as Homer.

thus also the space between Asia and Europe that Jupiter traverses as a bull, the Mediterranean Sea. This is a reminder that the epic expansiveness of the *Met.* is expressed both chronologically and spatially. It is a chronicle from the dawn of time to Ovid's day, but it is also a kind of world map, understood in Roman terms as an itinerary, converging progressively on the city of Rome. The end of the poem, prepared for by a spectacular approach to the city in the company of Aesculapius, god of medicine, relocated from his cult centre at Epidaurus in Greece in 291 BCE, brings Roman readers in around 8 CE to Rome and up to the present day.

But in both respects, chronological and geographical, the strong assertion of a comprehensible structure communicates what we should be finding in this poem, not what we consistently do. There is, in a very general sense, progress from then to now and there to here, but at any given point in the *Met.* we have precious little grasp of where we are or when. Many of the stories are told by characters within the poem, further imperilling any sense we have of its temporal progression or geographical location, and important ancient chronological markers like the fall of Troy are treated as incidental details. Creation itself arguably occurs three separate times in Books 1 and 2. In *Met.* 10, by way of illustration, we seem to be spending most of our time on the island of Cyprus, which is the backdrop for the tales of Pygmalion and Myrrha, who seduced her own father and turned into the myrrh tree. But in fact the narrative of the book ranges across the world, and is in any case a song sung by Orpheus, seated on a hillock in Thrace. Thus when we are reading of Venus trying to persuade her lover Adonis not to risk his life by hunting, Orpheus in Thrace sings about Venus in Arabia telling a story about Hippomenes and Atalanta in Greece. The geographical instability of the poem, always set against the expectation that all roads lead to Rome, is reflected in an abnormally peripatetic set of characters. Faced with an inherited contradiction in the myth of Niobe, the wife of a king of Thebes in central Greece associated with a rock on the slopes of Mt Sipylus near Izmir in modern Turkey, Ovid whips up a whirlwind and transports the petrified queen across to the other side of the Aegean Sea (6.310–12). We are not meant to miss what a desperate narrative strategy this is.

The route is irrational, if picturesque, then, and the speed is erratic, too, time stretching and contracting alarmingly. Sometimes the narrative lingers at length on a story, at others it travels at dizzying velocity through centuries. An epic predecessor of Ovid with an unusual interest in the passage of time, as we shall see in the *Fasti*, was Q. Ennius, author of the *Annales*, the national epic of Rome before it was superseded by Virgil's *Aeneid*.

There is a theory that Ennius initially organized his poem to cover exactly 1,000 years, from the fall of Troy in 1184 BCE to events in Rome in 184 BCE, a respect for orderly time singularly lacking from Ovid's poem. At the end of *Met.* 14 Ovid allows his narrative, at this point concerned with the death of Rome's first king Romulus and his and his wife's deification, to align itself with the conclusion of the first book of Ennius' *Annales*. Here the manipulation of book divisions implies that the entire remainder of Ennius' account of the glorious rise of Rome, all seventeen books, will be covered in just one book of the *Met.*, with a side implication, entirely apt, that the *Met.* is a kind of mirror-image of the *Annales*. In Books 12 to 15, as the poem approaches the present day, Ovid's narrative sets itself in explicit comparison with his epic predecessors, Homer's *Iliad* and Virgil's *Aeneid*, as he covers events during and immediately after the siege of Troy, and then Ennius' *Annales* when he moves on into Roman history—a backdrop against which his own idiosyncratic version of human history stands out sharply. That version deftly sidesteps any predictable material, or at least predictable material predictably treated: the episode of Dido, which extends from Book 1 to Book 4 of the *Aeneid*, the most popular episode in the poem according to Ovid himself (*Tristia* 2.533–6), is cheekily reduced to four lines (14.78–81): 'There Aeneas was received in her heart and home by Dido, | who would not bear well the departure of her Trojan husband; | and on a pyre made under the pretext of a sacrifice | fell on a sword, deceiving all as she had been deceived.' The narrative moves smartly on to the monkeys of Pithecusae.

Another example of Ovid's engagement with Virgil, his major point of reference, will illustrate the central importance of gender in Ovid's subversion of epic values, and also how Ovid likes to use the weight of the tradition against itself, in this case mining Virgil's poetry for material that will suit his unorthodox poetics. In *Aeneid* 11 Virgil gives a prominent role to the Amazonian warrior Camilla, a characterization recreated by Ovid in the huntress Atalanta, who joins a collection of conventionally male heroes in

Met. 8 to help Meleager dispatch a large and troublesome boar. But something that is marginal in Virgil's epic, the heroic activity of women, becomes focal to Ovid's narrative, and Ovid's departure is symbolized with dark humour. Camilla does not survive *Aeneid* 11, dying by a wound in her breast, the location of the wound underlining the anomalousness of her presence in the male world of epic. In Ovid, by contrast, it is a male warrior, Ancaeus, outraged by Atalanta's involvement, who vaunts the superiority of male over female fighting ability in an exaggerated display of bravado (to Ancaeus is attributed *temeraria uirtus*, which would be good Latin for 'toxic masculinity')—and is instantaneously dispatched by a blow from the boar in his groin. Ovid can use Virgil to define his own, alternative gender balance, but his intervention also advertises the subversive presence of figures like Camilla in Virgil's source text, respects in which the solid, dependable genre of epic may not be as stable as it imagines it is. This is Ovid as literary hooligan.

The hero, the amplified male protagonist embodying power and authority, stands at the very heart of epic poetry, and here and elsewhere is a favourite target for Ovid. The greatest epic hero was Achilles, but his death was never directly described in the formative epics of antiquity. The subject suits Ovid's purposes both for that reason and because it comes at the hands of a character, Paris, whose heroic credentials are questionable, and who delivers the fatal wound by the inadequately heroic means of an arrow shot. 'And so, conqueror of so many men, Achilles,' comments the poet, 'You were conquered by the cowardly thief of a Greek wife; | but if you had had to die by womanly arms, | you would rather have fallen by the double axe of the Amazon' (12.608–11). The Amazon Penthesilea (a model for Camilla and Atalanta) had come to the aid of Troy after the episode covered by Homer's *Iliad*: a celebrated sculpture group depicted Achilles falling in love with her after he had delivered the blow that killed her. The idea in Ovid that Achilles might have welcomed defeat at a woman's hands cuts away at his heroic status, of course, but so also does the erotic motive. Time and again in this poem heroic action is disrupted by the elegiac motive of love, starting with the moment when Phoebus Apollo, flushed with his first manly exploit, the slaying of the monster Python at Delphi, suffers the intervention of his brother Cupid, who makes him fall in love with Daphne, and Daphne want absolutely nothing to do with him (1.438–567). Cupid had done exactly the same to Ovid himself in the first poem of the *Amores*, compelling the poet to fall in love and write love-elegy, or rather write love-elegy and fall in love, by stealing a foot from his second line and making him an elegiac poet; Apollo in the *Met.* has gone from epic hero to elegiac lover.

Another hero illustrates a different way, a particularly delightful one, in which the inherently masculine ethos of epic might be punctured. Book 9 introduces to the poem the very greatest hero of them all, Hercules. But while his famous Twelve Labours are a regular point of reference, Ovid once again expertly avoids any direct engagement with anything so conventionally heroic. 'Labour' in Latin is *labor*, and the word features regularly in the narrative to denote a heroic Labour. But the episode to which Ovid rapidly plots his way deploys the word in a markedly different sense, the (in its own way) truly epic seven-day labour (*labor* again in Latin) by which Hercules' mother Alcmene had given birth to the hero. The outcome of the story, told by Alcmene herself, is the transformation into the weasel of a servant called Galanthis, who had cleverly ensured that Alcmene would be allowed to give birth to Hercules in the face of Juno's resistance. Weasels had the domestic status in antiquity, as mousers, that cats or dogs do today: 'She is busy about my house,' Alcmene concludes, 'just as she was before' (9.323), and the shift of perspective from the heroic to the small-scale and domestic is complete.

James Joyce's *A Portrait of the Artist as a Young Man*, which introduces the semi-autobiographical character Stephen Dedalus, has as its epigraph *Met.* 8.188, *et ignotas animum dimittit in artes*, 'and Daedalus set his mind to arts unknown'. Joyce, famously, claimed to have included enough 'enigmas and puzzles' in *Ulysses* to 'keep the professors busy for centuries arguing over what I meant', and the appeal of the Roman poet to the Irish novelist is not far to seek. Ovid sets the reader Joycean intellectual challenges, but also like Joyce he was aware of the melancholy truth that his poem would rapidly find its way into the hands of captious professors. That emerges from a comparison of the guiding metaphor of his critics, on the one hand, and a prominent motif in the poem, on the other. The critics are unanimous that Ovid is immature, childish: the 'schoolboy silliness', *pueriles ineptiae*, of Seneca and Dryden's 'boyisms', but also Quintilian's *lasciuus*, 'mischievous'. But there is a discernible tendency within Ovid's poem, too, for childish figures to obstruct heroic activity. Here is Daedalus manufacturing the wings that carry himself and his son Icarus away from Crete (8.188–200):

> So Daedalus spoke, and turns his mind to unknown arts,
> and transforms nature. For he places feathers in a row,
> as if they had grown naturally in ascending size; just so does
> a rustic pipe gradually increase with reeds of unequal length.
> Then he binds them with twine and wax at the middle and base,
> and when so arranged, bends them with a slight curve
> to mimic real birds. The boy Icarus was alongside him
> standing there and, unaware he was handling his own demise,
> with shining face now snatched at the feathers moved
> by the shifting breeze, now moulded the yellow wax
> with his thumb, and by his play hindered the marvellous
> work of his father.

The wondrous achievement of Daedalus, on the one hand, and Icarus' childish inability to resist interfering, on the other (Icarus' mischievous disobedience will shortly be the death of him), are hard not to read as a self-reflexive expression of the *Met.*'s deep poetics, the *lasciuia*, playfulness, that disrupts the heroic action proper to the form. If so, though, Ovid has identified and deployed the metaphor for which Seneca, Quintilian, and Dryden will reach to find fault with his poetry, and his ability to anticipate the terms of his own criticism is not the least indication of his genius.

Two further thoughts on this passage, the first metrical. Epic, as we have seen, is more or less synonymous with its characteristic metre, the heroic hexameter. If Ovid is abusing epic convention here, it's noticeable that Icarus' intervention ('The boy Icarus . . . work of his father') also disrupts heroic form, coming in halfway through a hexametrical line, and ending halfway through another: in each case denying the heroic line its integrity. (I have tried to mimic the effect in my translation.) On the other hand, and in contrast to that very formal observation, there is another layer to this piece of self-commentary that should not be neglected. It is a metaliterary vignette, replete with significance for the poem to which it belongs, but it is at the same time a vividly realistic scene, the universally recognizable circumstance of a child refusing to behave, chasing feathers.

'This poem has been ever since the magazine which has furnished the greatest poets of the following ages with fancy, and allusions; and the most celebrated paintings with subjects and designs'—the words of Samuel Garth, who coordinated a translation of the *Met.* 'by the most Eminent Hands' which was published in 1717 (Preface, p. xviii). One of the hands whose work Garth included in his volume was John Dryden, hitherto presented in this book as a stern critic of the *Met.*, though keener on the *Heroides*. It is perhaps more accurate to see in Dryden an embodiment of the deep ambivalence that Ovid has always seemed to provoke, and his masterpiece the *Met.* in particular. By the time Dryden wrote the translations that Samuel Garth reused (some years after his death), Dryden was a marginalized figure, a Catholic and Jacobite who had been expelled from his role as Poet Laureate, and on one occasion at least Ovid provided him with an opportunity for a most Ovidian expression of nonconformity. In Book 1 of the *Met.* a Council of the Gods is called by Jupiter to discuss what to do with a humanity that had become hopelessly corrupt. Of Jupiter's heavenly palace, where the gods convene, Ovid writes: 'This is the place which, if boldness were lent to my words, | I should not fear to speak of as great heaven's Palatine' (1.175–6), comparing heaven with Augustus' house (the original 'palace') on the Palatine hill. George Sandys's 1626 translation was dedicated to Charles I, and Charles's palace in London loyally replaces the Palatine: 'This glorious Roofe I would not doubt to call, | Had I but boldnesse lent mee, Heauen's *White-Hall*.' Dryden, in contrast, mischievously implies that no English building could fit the bill: 'This place, as far as Earth with Heav'n may vie, | I dare to call the Louvre of the skie', an arresting choice given the French king's support for the Jacobite cause.

Dryden's strictures against Ovid's irreverence elsewhere ('if this were wit, was this a time to be witty, when the poor wretch was in the agony of death?') were not unparalleled, and indeed the 'Augustan Age' from which Garth's collection emerged was one of the least sympathetic to the anti-classical tendencies of the *Met.* But if the popularity of the poem has ebbed and flowed, its intrinsic variety has also allowed markedly different times and values to see their reflection within it. This is a poem that can provoke engagements as diverse, yet also in their way entirely true to their model, as Ali Smith's novel *Girl Meets Boy* (2007) and *Titus Andronicus*. Shakespeare's affinity for Ovid is familiar, the *Met.* his favourite classical poem, albeit sometimes mediated by Golding's English translation of 1567. It has been suggested that Ovidian influence is most strongly felt in plays 'concerned with art itself, especially the art of words, and the relationship of imagination and reality' (Caroline Jameson).

In *Titus Andronicus*, Shakespeare (perhaps in collaboration with another author) sets out to both imitate and surpass one of Ovid's most grisly tales, the rape of Philomela by Tereus in *Met.* 6, and the killing and cooking of Tereus' son Itys that eventuated. After raping Philomela, Tereus had cut out her tongue to prevent her incriminating him, but Philomela managed to communicate the truth to Procne (her sister, Tereus' wife and Itys' mother) by weaving a tapestry of the scene. In *Titus Andronicus* Lavinia's hands are cut off as well as her tongue as if consciously to preclude Philomela's solution. Lavinia's means of revealing the crime is explicitly Ovidian, turning the pages of 'Ovid's *Metamorphosis*' to the relevant story: 'Soft, so busily she turns the leaves! | What would she find? Lavinia, shall I read? | This is the tragic tale of Philomel . . .' (4.1.45–7). What the author of *Titus Andronicus* found in Ovid was inspiration for an astonishingly bloodthirsty drama, graphic violence successfully packaged as entertainment. Yet not a whit less true to the shifting character of the *Met.* is Smith's *Girl Meets Boy*, a delightful retelling of Iphis and Ianthe in contemporary Scotland, authentically light and mischievous, and as warm-hearted in the way it resolves the gender dilemma that Ovid had solved through metamorphosis as *Titus* is darkly relentless in its emulation of Tereus.

Ovid's Philomela, indeed, has been the focus of much contemporary anxiety about the *Met.* In some respects, as we have seen, Ovid might be seen as a remarkably liberal voice to emerge from a patriarchal society like Rome. But sexual violence against women is a recurrent feature of the poem, rape by definition the lot of mortal women, as Caenis suggests (12.202) when she requests from her rapist Neptune metamorphosis into a man named Caeneus so as not to have to suffer rape a second time.

Gian Lorenzo Bernini (1598–1680) has a status in the plastic arts comparable to Shakespeare in literature, and also displayed a comparable sympathy for Ovid (or Ovidian myth: we must allow again for a richly mediated tradition), reflected in his famous sculptural group *Apollo and Daphne*, which (as originally positioned) presents to the viewer moving around the statue not so much the moment of Daphne's metamorphosis into the laurel tree as a narrative of metamorphosis in stone, hair turning into leaves, skin to bark. A study of the potential of stone to represent reality, *Apollo and Daphne* is also a challenge to poetic efforts such as Ovid's to depict metamorphosis in words: which of these media of representation was more adept was a live issue in Bernini's circles. But it is no coincidence that the process of metamorphosis becomes the arena for a display of creative art, given the affinity between artistic representation and metamorphosis that we have already noted. In the case of another celebrated sculpture by Bernini, the *Rape of Persephone*, he achieves the remarkable effect in marble of flesh pressed by the hand of Pluto as he abducts the girl. Again sculpture flaunts its powers of illusion, but in this case what is also shared with Ovid is a readiness to make art of sexual violence, notwithstanding a Renaissance viewer's readiness to moralize the scene.

Teasing out Ovid's influence from the multiple sources that Bernini or other artists had for such myths is hard. To trace the figure of Narcissus through visual art, literature, and beyond is to see an Ovidian creation so powerfully realized that it has long since escaped any close association with Ovid's poem. Salvador Dalí showed his surrealist *Metamorphosis of Narcissus* (Figure 6)

6. *Metamorphosis of Narcissus* by Salvador Dalí.

to Sigmund Freud, and the conversation was a very 20th-century one about the human mind. Ovid deserves credit, nevertheless, for the realization of a fictional character sufficiently compelling to achieve this cultural autonomy.

And that in itself points to the most striking, and paradoxical, legacy of the *Met.*, that the versions of these folktales presented in Ovid's poem, shaped as they were by the literary tastes of Ovid's day, but above all by the sheer joyous idiosyncrasy of this poet, have escaped the poem and lived on independently. Sometimes these are indeed identified as stories that originate in Ovid's *Metamorphoses*, but as often as not they are simply described as 'Greek Mythology'.

Chapter 5
The *Fasti*

The *Fasti* is Ovid's most topical poem, in the sense of being directly engaged with the religious, and hence political, culture of the city, and its sacred and secular topography—and necessarily also with the specific conditions of Augustan Rome. It may indicate a belated awareness on Ovid's part that the emperor was worth cultivating.

This all follows from the subject that Ovid had selected: *Fasti* means 'The Calendar'. Strictly speaking, *(dies) fasti* are 'the days on which it is allowable to speak' (Varro, *De Lingua Latina* 6.29–30), to be even more precise days on which an official called the *praetor urbanus* could adjudicate legal cases. But the term came to denote a calendar in its peculiarly Roman form: a document recording the eight-day ('nundinal') market cycle, the status of each day (the letter F against a day for *fastus*, for example; N for *nefastus*, the opposite), the Kalends, Nones, and Ides that punctuated each month, and in addition the major state festivals and other festive and significant days, especially the foundation dates of temples, as they fell through the year. Surviving Roman calendars include the republican *Fasti Antiates* found at Anzio and the imperial *Fasti Praenestini* from Palestrina (see Figure 7), the latter compiled by the eminent Augustan scholar M. Verrius Flaccus. Flaccus' antiquarian research, and Ovid's in this poem, echo the emperor's interest in the Roman past, reflected in his

7. A section of the *Fasti Praenestini*, recording the end of April (including the festival of Flora, which ran on into May).

revival of obsolete traditions and dilapidated temples, related in turn to his moral legislation. Indeed a noteworthy recent addition to the calendar in Ovid's day had been commemorative material related to Augustus and his family, a development that did not go uncontested (the later historian Tacitus talks of 'the *fasti* befouled by flattery', *Hist.* 4.40). All in all the *Fasti* is an Ovidian poem for those who like their flippancy cut with a fair dose of fascinating cultural minutiae.

Ovid's poem presents itself as a poetic version of a document like the *Fasti Praenestini*. Since our year, the twelve months and their names and lengths, is inherited from the Romans, the broader structure of his poem is familiar to us. Each book corresponds to a month (though in the event Ovid only published January to June), and each month is divided up into accounts, varying in length from a passing reference to a few hundred verses, of individual days. The content that Ovid includes is justified, sometimes contentiously, by the ritual or rituals associated with each day. Ovid likes to appear constrained in the material he can associate with any given day, but the wealth of Roman religious observance, allied with Ovid's own inventiveness, gives him all the resources of Greek myth and Roman history to bring to the poem. Thus 'a tale full of ancient jest' (2.304) on the occasion of the Lupercalia on 15 February tells of Hercules swapping clothes with his lover Omphale and confusing the aggressively oversexed Faunus-Pan. On the Ides of March the festival of Anna Perenna allows Ovid to describe the arrival of Dido's sister Anna in Italy, the jealousy of Aeneas' wife Lavinia, and Anna's escape out of a window—a plot straight out of the Adultery Mime (3.543–656). The 11th of June features the abominable princess Tullia, driving in her carriage over her father's corpse, along what was as a result in Ovid's day called *vicus Sceleratus*, 'Wicked Street' (6.585–620). On 23 March we learn of the complex origin of the Golden Fleece, the escape of Phrixus and Helle on a flying ram from the plots of their stepmother with the help of their real, dead mother who saw what was happening to them, Ovid archly remarks, 'as by chance she hung in the sky'. Their mother's name (Ovid leaves us to work out) was Nephele, whose name means 'cloud' in Greek (3.851–76).

The first and last of these examples are illustrations of Greek myth (unexpectedly) incorporated into this Roman calendar-poem, and also of material generated exclusively from an astronomical observation, in this case the sun entering the zodiacal sign of the Ram. An apparent departure by Ovid from the model of Roman calendars is his regular reference to such material, especially the rising and setting of stars, and accompanying meteorological information. *Tempora cum causis Latium digesta per annum | lapsaque sub terras ortaque signa canam*, the poem begins (1.1–2): 'Of time arranged across the Latin year | and constellations that have set beneath the earth and risen I shall sing.' In fact the stellar material clarifies the inspiration of his poem. What made the calendar a compelling topic for Augustan Romans was the radical reform that Julius Caesar, the adoptive father of Augustus, had introduced from 45 BCE, whereby a civil year that had been disorientatingly out of kilter with the natural year was restored to harmony: 46 BCE was 'the last year of confusion', in the words of Macrobius, *Sat.* 1.14.3, and needed to last a total of 445 days to ensure that harvest festivals came in the summer and celebration of the vintage in the autumn, to paraphrase the biographer Suetonius (*Life of Julius Caesar* 40.1). By reconciling the cycles of the moon and the solar year (bar some tweaking of leap years by Pope Gregory in the 16th century) Caesar had in fact established the conditions in which the material of a *parapegma* (as a calendrical list of stellar and meteorological phenomena was known), the risings and settings of constellations, could be mapped securely onto a human calendar. (Indeed it seems that Caesar published a *parapegma* of his own in association with this reform.) It should be added that Ovid's astronomical material, in the past assumed to be wildly inaccurate, is sound enough by ancient standards.

An interest in the administration of time, and its implications for civic order more widely, was one among many things that Augustus inherited from his adoptive father. In 9–8 BCE Augustus introduced a recalibration of the Julian year (intercalation of days had not been properly observed in the years since 45 BCE), renamed the month of Sextilis 'Augustus' (Quinctilis had become 'Julius' in 45), and unveiled an enormous monument in the Campus Martius the precise function of which is disputed—but it bore some relation to a sundial, with a twenty-metre-tall Egyptian obelisk as its gnomon: a confidence that one's reforms will last the distance has rarely been more boldly expressed. An important prerequisite both of Caesar's epochal reform and Augustus' fine-tuning, and one that tells us something about Romans' perception of the calendar, is that it was carried out in both cases in their role as Pontifex Maximus, the chief priest of Rome. In fact the strange delay on Augustus' part, leaving a reform so obviously necessary until twenty years after he achieved uncontested power, is explained by his need to wait for the previous Pontifex, M. Aemilius Lepidus, to die and leave the position vacant. In Rome, in other words, the administration of time was an essentially religious task, and any poem that tackles the topic of the calendar is in consequence concerning itself with issues fundamental to Rome's religion, sacred landscape, and past and present as united in ritual time—in short, with Roman identity.

The *Fasti* has in the past been read too straight—as a sober delineation of Roman religious life. J. G. Frazer, the scholar of religion also responsible for *The Golden Bough*, published a monumental five-volume edition of the poem in 1929. The *Fasti* is more playful and elusive than that, but there are nonetheless moments (a merchant's self-serving prayer to Mercury, god of trade and trickery, at 5.675–92, is one example) where we are perhaps close to an authentic impression of Roman religiosity. A medieval legend incidentally had it that the missing last six books of the poem had been destroyed by St Jerome, a figure strongly associated with the transition from a pagan to a Christian culture, for their idolatrous subject matter. Much later there developed a thriving genre of Christian *Fasti*, modelled on Ovid's poem while playing off its pagan religious content. Thus the 16th-century poet Ambrogio Fracco, known as 'Novidius', 'New Ovid', adopted one of Ovid's scholarly explanations of the name 'April', from Latin *aperire*, 'to open' (the 'opening' of the year in spring), but rejects his pagan account and suggests instead a source in the 'opened tomb' of Christ at Easter.

But if the *Fasti* is tackling an essentially religious subject, the Roman calendar and its recent history were to Ovid inspiration for a poem that combines religion, myth, history, and contemporary observation with all the poetic self-awareness that we associate with his style. If that sounds quite a lot like the *Metamorphoses*, these texts are indeed closely, even symbiotically, related. Both poems are fundamentally interested in time, albeit in the *Met.* a linear time from Creation to the present day, and in the *Fasti* the cyclic time of the year. According to an established convention in Roman poetry, the first word or words of a poem functioned as its alternative title (Virgil's *Aeneid* was often 'Arms and the man', for example). Since the *Fasti*'s first word is *tempora*, 'times', another way of reading Ovid's request to the gods at the start of the *Metamorphoses* to lead his song from the origin of the universe 'to my times', *ad mea tempora*, is that the conclusion of the chronology of that poem connects with the cyclical time of the *Fasti*. The poems were certainly being composed more or less concurrently in the years leading up to his exile in 8 or 9 CE.

Elsewhere we are encouraged to read variations of the same story in *Metamorphoses* and *Fasti* against each other, notably the goddess Ceres' quest for her abducted daughter Persephone in *Met.* 5 and *Fasti* 4. The implication is that there are meaningful differences in the treatment of the story between the poems, and the roots of the divergence are generic and metrical. The *Met.* is composed in epic verse, dactylic hexameters, but in the *Fasti* Ovid reverts to his default metre, elegiac couplets. With Ceres this translates into an epic portrayal of the goddess in the *Met.*, driven by the classic epic motive of anger; and a mournful figure in the *Fasti* (the association of elegy and lament being activated here). Now, this is Ovid, and in the *Fasti*, no less than the *Met.*, there is a commitment to generic instability, a determination to test and challenge the formal character he has in each case adopted. A striking moment in the *Fasti* is when Ceres expresses her grief with a reaction that is inappropriate to, indeed (Ovid insists) inconceivable for, a divine being (4.521–2): 'The goddess spoke, and like tears (for gods cannot weep) | a gleaming drop fell onto her warm breast.' What is it that drops from Ceres' eye, exactly? Not a tear, because gods cannot experience mortal grief; yet Ceres is a character in elegy, and elegy, according to one traditional association, is the very genre of grief. What happens to Ceres is physiologically incomprehensible, but as such it expresses the distilled essence of another brilliantly elusive poem.

The metrical form of the *Fasti*, the elegiacs that seem to interrupt the poetry every second line, entails, as we have considered before, a further set of formal expectations: brevity and discontinuity of expression, in particular. An example of elegiac concision comes from the start of March, a superbly brisk list of parallels from other Italian calendars for honouring the god Mars with a month's name (3.87–96):

> If you have any leisure, have a look at foreign calendars:
> > in them too there will be a month named for Mars.
> It was the third month in the Alban calendar, fifth in the Faliscan,
> > sixth among your peoples, land of the Hernicans.
> Between the Aricini and the calendar of Alba there is agreement,
> > so too the walls built high by the hand of Telegonus.
> It is fifth for the Laurentes, twice fifth for the vigorous Aequiculan,
> > the first after the third for the people of Cures;
> and you, bellicose Paelignian, agree with your Sabine ancestors:
> > the god comes fourth for both these peoples.

The division of each month into days, themselves sometimes divided into multiple accounts reflecting the unrelated cultic associations of any given day, ensures an essentially disjointed narrative thread within the book. Nothing is more discontinuous than the passage from day to night, after all, especially when organized in the manner of civic time. On the other hand, though, nothing (regrettably) is more relentless than time, either. Ovid's poem represents a *series rerum*, 'a chain of events', that he must never break (1.62): the *Fasti*, he implies, is identical with the year it depicts, subject to the same irresistible progress. Day is indeed defined by night, but another day inevitably follows: 'Time [*tempora*, so the *Fasti*, too] slips away, and we grow old as the years pass silently: | no delaying bridle curbs the days as they flee' (6.771–2).

This tension between discontinuity and continuity, familiar to us from the *Metamorphoses*, is even embodied in the text on the page. Modern editors, in an effort to make the poem easier to follow, have separated the days out into paragraphs, prefacing them with calendrical material from inscribed *fasti*—a letter indicating the nundinal day, and further letters like F or N indicating the status of the day. In effect this makes each day of the *Fasti* something like an individual poem, and each book of the *Fasti* more like a book of the *Amores*. Once again, scholars distant in time from Ovid are allowing him to manipulate them: since each day tends to focus on new material unrelated to what precedes or follows, there is a compulsion to distinguish them. But in fact this modern intervention radically falsifies the Ovidian text and the reading practice it encouraged. In its original form the *Fasti* offered an unbroken text from start to finish of each book, without any editorial material indicating day divisions, insisting on continuity even as the reader experiences the unpredictability of day succeeding to day. It follows that the *Fasti* offered unique challenges to its ancient as well as its modern readers.

As in the *Metamorphoses*, this formal issue is bound up with the collision of higher and lower poetic genres. The clearest model for a poem explaining in antiquarian style the origins of Roman festivals is Callimachus' *Aetia* ('Causes'), his elegiac poem recounting the origins of (mainly) religious practices. As in the *Fasti*, episodes in the *Aetia* varied significantly in length and bore a tenuous relationship to their neighbours. Callimachus' own self-proclaimed model, the archaic Greek poet Hesiod, is another presence in Ovid's poem (when he is addressed by the god Janus as *uates operose dierum*, 'hard*working* poet of *days*' (1.101), there is an allusion to the name of Hesiod's poem *Works and Days*), as is Aratus, a contemporary of Callimachus (and praised by him, *inter alia* as a follower of Hesiod), who offers a literary precedent for Ovid's astronomical and meteorological lore. Altogether, this cluster of associations locates the *Fasti* firmly in a tradition of Hellenistic didactic poetry, and other aspects of the poem confirm this affiliation. It takes the form of a personal account of research undertaken by a scholarly persona, thereby closely imitating Callimachus' self-presentation in the *Aetia*. The element of teaching is reminiscent of the *Ars Amatoria*, but the *Fasti* is not mock-didactic in the same way, even if at times Ovid pokes fun at the antiquarian research he claims to be pursuing. 'For sure I myself have leapt over the flames placed three in a row,' he claims, while describing the Parilia on 21 April, and the incongruity of the bookish scholar-poet getting properly involved in the peculiar rustic ritual is undoubtedly meant to be amusing.

But what is much less Callimachean about the *Fasti* is its focus on something so intrinsically nationalistic (the natural territory of epic) as the Roman calendar. The *Aetia* had had its panegyrical moments—Books 3–4 were seemingly framed by praises of Berenice, queen of Egypt, for example—but Ovid's material, Rome's history and its current rulers, inevitably draws the poem toward a higher literary register. Q. Ennius, author of the epic *Annales* (and expert on time), is another significant point of reference, and when at the very start of the poem Ovid promises Germanicus (the adoptive son, and heir, of the emperor Tiberius to whom he rededicated the poem while in exile), 'You will rediscover festivals unearthed from ancient annals, | and how each day earned its notation,' 'annals' hints at Ennius' poem as well as a very official and dry variety of Roman historical record. It is no coincidence either that a complete *Fasti*, covering January to December, would have contained twelve books and thereby been an elegiac rival to Virgil's epic on the history of Rome. The tension in the *Fasti* between *Aetia* and *Aeneid*, its elegiac and epic impulses, is of course entirely deliberate.

A passage from Book 4 will serve to illustrate some of the complex of threads that feed into Ovid's calendar poem. It starts on 6 April, the third day of a festival of the goddess Magna Mater known as the *Megalesia*, and Ovid shares a personal anecdote from the theatre performances that marked the festival. By virtue of one of the political offices he had held as a young man, he finds himself in the privileged seating alongside a man who had achieved high rank in warfare:

> It was the third day of the games, I recall, and an
>   old man, sitting next me as I watched,
> said to me, 'This is the day when Caesar on Libyan shores
>   crushed the treacherous forces of noble Juba.   380
> Caesar was my commander; under him I am proud
>   to have served as tribune: he it was bestowed my commission.
> This seat I got in war, you in peace,
>   by virtue of holding office on the Board of Ten.'
> We were about to speak further, but a shower of rain separated us: 385
>   The Scales hanging in the sky were releasing their waters.
> But before the last day puts an end to the shows,
>   sword-bearing Orion will be sunk in the sea.
> When the next dawn gazes upon victorious Rome,
>   and the stars in flight given way to the Sungod,   390
> the Circus will be thronged with a procession and a parade of gods,
>   and horses, as quick as the wind, will compete for the winning palm.

We travel in this passage from 6 to 10 April. In modern texts it is broken up as the days change at 387 (9 April) and 389 (10 April), but presented as Ovid intended, uninterrupted, it becomes clear that there is a narrative thread that works in pleasing counterpoint to the division by days: the account of 6 April is interrupted by rain, then Orion (a constellation believed to herald rainfall) sets by the time of the 9th (the rain eases, in other words), and morning sunshine greets the horseracing on the 10th.

But if we focus on 6 April, Ovid's encounter with the veteran (377–86), it has the elegiac character of a personal anecdote, the researcher revealing something of himself, and there is in fact an allusion to Callimachus here: in a surviving fragment of the *Aetia* (fr. 178), now thought to originate in Book 2, Callimachus described how at a feast he learned from a merchant named Theogenes, 'with whom I shared a couch', about the worship of the hero Peleus on his home island of Icus. At the same time, though, Ovid's veteran talks of war and politics, the stuff of epic, and it is only the intervention of rain (or you might say, the Aratean material of astronomy and weather) that prevents a full-blown account of the Battle of Thapsus in 46 BCE from the loquacious old soldier.

In other words, Ovid's encounter at the theatre is rather like Icarus playing in Daedalus' workshop, a vignette expressive of the deep character of the composition, in this case a poem hovering at the edge of the capacities of elegiac form. But like Icarus again, and this is just as important, it is a vivid scene that Ovid is painting, a persuasive account of human interaction. It is grounded in Roman realities, and the old veteran is characterized by his speech, its military language, pride, and nostalgia. Line 383, 'This seat I got in war, you in peace', in Latin *hanc ego militia sedem tu pace parasti*, has a balance that captures beautifully Ovid and the retired soldier sharing a seat side by side, but encapsulates also the divided poetics of the *Fasti*, delicately poised between peace and war.

It may be worth adding that Ovid's account of the *Megalesia*, mainly delivered to the poet by the Muse Erato, is an intensely Callimachean episode: the first two books of the *Aetia* apparently took the form of a dream in which Callimachus was informed by the Muses on Mt Helicon of the *aetia* or causes that his poem described. One of many open questions about Callimachus' poem is how the episode of Theogenes of Icus fitted into that exchange between Callimachus and the Muses. But I suspect that Ovid's sequence of a human interlocutor after a Muse would look even more Callimachean if we possessed more of Callimachus' hugely influential poem. (Such is the speculative nature of literary analysis when many of the texts we'd like to have, in this case the *Aetia* and *Annales*, are in fragments!)

The dilemma between war and peace glimpsed in this anecdote is in fact very central to the thematics of the *Fasti*. 'Let others sing of Caesar's weapons,' Ovid proclaims in Book 1: 'I shall sing of Caesar's altars.' The weapons, *arma*, put us in mind of the opening of Virgil's epic *Aeneid*, *arma uirumque*, 'Arms and the man'. An association of elegy with peace, meanwhile, followed from its established opposition to epic poetry, stereotypically preoccupied with war. But on closer inspection this firm distinction between war and peace, epic and elegy, is less clear-cut than it seems. Both weapons and altars are Caesar's, after all, and between the Latin words *arma* and *arae* there is barely a letter's difference. Furthermore, since the establishment of cults in Rome was typically a consequence of military victory, even altars are bound to involve the poet in military matters. The presiding deity of the year and this poem, double-faced Janus, with whom Ovid converses at length on his feast day, 1 January (1.63–288), is a god of peace—the doors of his temple in the Roman Forum were shut whenever peace was achieved across the empire, something Augustus ostentatiously did three times. But it is a very Roman notion of peace that Janus embodies, *pax* achieved by military *pacification*, the violent defeat of enemies: 'Attend with favour our generals,' Ovid prays to him, 'by whose toil | the fruitful earth and the sea enjoy peace' (1.67–8).

A representative moment comes on 3 June (6.199–208), the anniversary of the consecration of the temple of the war-god Bellona in the Campus Martius. By a typical process, this temple had been vowed by a celebrated figure of the Roman past, Appius Claudius the Blind (the builder of the Appian Way), during a war with a combined force of Etruscans and Samnites, and then realized after the goddess had granted him victory. In front of this temple stood a low pillar ('a small column of no small significance') from which a priest known as a Fetial threw a spear as a symbolic way of declaring war. In describing this cult site Ovid himself approaches to the very brink of warfare without quite engaging in poetic combat.

If war/peace, *arma*/*arae* and epic/elegy are concepts that map neatly onto one another and represent important creative tensions within the *Fasti*, two more comparable dichotomies are male/female and Romulus/Numa Pompilius. To start with the latter, the first two kings of Rome, legendary rather than truly historical, were felt to represent a polarity of their own, the militaristic Romulus providing the nascent city with security, while Numa followed up with the gentler forms of civilization, religious observance especially: 'At first the Romans were too ready to resort to arms: | Numa resolved to soften them with law and fear of the gods. | Hence laws were established, so that the stronger man might not be all-powerful, | and rites handed down began to be properly observed' (3.277–80). Numa, pious and scholarly, and in general a model for the poet of the *Fasti* himself, in effect made the *Fasti* possible, and he features regularly in it, one extended example being the focus on Vesta, goddess of hearth and home and by extension of the Roman people as a whole, at 6.249–468 (the festival of the Vestalia on 9 June). The temple of Vesta in the Forum was both the very heart of Roman religious observance, site of a flame that must never be extinguished, and also originally Numa's palace.

Romulus the warrior is also a regular presence in the poem, but a much less assured figure when he is. Ovid regularly hints that the first king of Rome was more brawn than brain. Responsible for an originally ten-month year (once again it is Numa who raised them to the proper twelve), 'Evidently, Romulus, you were more familiar with warfare (*arma*) than stars, | and conquering neighbours was your greater concern' (1.29–30). There have been attempts to read Ovid's preference for Numa, and characterization of Romulus as a bit thick, as a subtle critique of the emperor, and it is true that Augustus cultivated an association with Romulus: his very name, adopted at the formal establishment of the terms of his rule in 27 BCE, partly derives from Ennius' description of Rome's foundation in his *Annales*—the *augustum augurium*, 'venerable omen', of twelve eagles which gave Romulus the right to build it. In truth, however, Augustus put as much energy into cultivating his image as a second Numa. His whole programme of moral and religious renovation was strongly Numan in inspiration, one example being the emphasis he placed on closing the gates of the temple of Janus, one of Numa's most celebrated foundations. I have also stressed the importance of Augustus' status as Pontifex Maximus, emulating his adoptive father Caesar's calendrical reforms in the role of the chief priest. Numa was the first Pontifex Maximus, and any incumbent of the chief priesthood in Rome was to Numa what the Pope is to St Peter. That said, Ovid's clear favouring of one aspect of Augustus' complex self-presentation (and exaggeration of the Romulus–Numa polarity) may not have been entirely politic.

Elsewhere, the poet's trademark mischievousness can certainly extend to hints of political subversion. They may require some paranoid reading to draw them out, but it has been pointed out that Augustus' later reign, struck as it was by a series of misfortunes that threatened to unpick the emperor's careful arrangements for the future, and characterized by increasing repression of opposing views, was a paranoid time: Ovid himself would feel the consequences. On 24 February a long account of the rape of Lucretia, the consequence of which was the expulsion of the kings and establishment of a free republic, ends: 'Tarquin and his children are exiled, and a consul assumes yearly | jurisdiction: that was the last day for kingship' (*Fasti* 2.851-2). Ovid then moves on to 'parapegmatic' material: 'Am I wrong, or has the swallow come, harbinger of spring, | and does she not fear that winter may turn and come again?' (2.853-4). In a text with the peculiar formal characteristics of the *Fasti*, however, continuous and discontinuous simultaneously, moments of transition are unusually hard to fix. In this environment there is an exquisitely subtle note of doubt ('Am I wrong?') momentarily attached, at least, to the claim that, with the establishment of the Roman Republic in 509 BCE, monarchy was forever banished from the city. It mattered to Augustus to dissemble the real control that he exerted over Rome, and to claim that he represented a continuation of the notionally democratic politics of the Republic, but the pretence that he was anything but an autocrat was wearing very thin. Such moments should nevertheless be set in the context of much material in the *Fasti* that it is hard to read as anything but unqualified panegyric of Augustus and his family. The very subject of the poem is unthinkable without the calendrical activities of the Julians.

The beginnings of Books 3 and 4, March and April, form a doublet, two eponymous gods, Mars and Venus, who were also in a famous myth adulterous lovers, standing in sharp contrast to one another. Mars, the war god, cuts a superbly awkward figure at the start of Book 3, prepared to take his helmet off while in Ovid's poem, but clinging nervously to his spear (3.171-2). Venus in Book 4, in contrast, a female goddess with a foundational role in Rome's mythic origins, matches more comfortably the complex poetics of the poem. Taking its lead from the goddess, the book of April pursues another impulse of elegy, a metre and genre conventionally gendered feminine, and delivers a feminized version of Roman history. It is Erato, Muse of love poetry, who explains to the poet the festival of the Magna Mater, and one consequence is the foregrounding of a woman's role in the establishment of the cult two centuries before. That woman is Claudia Quinta, portrayed by Ovid, or rather Erato, as a confident, outgoing character somewhat reminiscent of the mistress of love-elegy. Claudia is suspected of unchastity, but Ovid depicts her triumphantly vindicating her good character by performing a miracle, releasing the ship carrying the image of the Magna Mater to Rome from a sandbank in the river Tiber. The limelight enjoyed by Claudia in Erato's narrative, furthermore, comes at the cost of a superlative man. An alternative version of the arrival of the Magna Mater, probably the more mainstream one, involved the identification of an 'ideal man', *optimus uir*, suitable to receive the image of the goddess. The historian Livy's account of this event (29.11.5–9, 14.5–14) is mainly about the selection of P. Cornelius Scipio Nasica as worthy of this momentous role, and Claudia is sidelined. But Erato dismisses Scipio's involvement in two words, *Nasica accepit*, 'Nasica received her' (347)—in fact, since the vowels ending and beginning words coalesce in Roman verse, in five syllables, *Nasicaccepit*, a fraction of a heroic line.

One of the most appealing passages of the *Fasti*, the account of the Floralia, the festival of Flora, goddess of flowering (of crops as well as flowers), in Book 5, carries a similar implication of the femininity of this elegiac text. (It lies behind some of the imagery of Botticelli's famous painting *Primavera*.) There is a particular warmth to Ovid's narrative of this festival, a time associated with *lasciuia maior* | . . . *liberiorque iocus*, 'a greater naughtiness | . . . and more permissive play' (5.331–2), and to his interactions with the spring goddess herself, as if she answers especially well to the character of his poem, a Roman god with elegiac sensibilities: 'She had finished her story; she vanished into thin air. | Her scent lingered: you would know a goddess had been there. | That the song of Naso may bloom for all time, | scatter, I pray, your gifts upon my breast' (375–8). Since Ovid's name 'Naso' means 'Big nose', Flora's fragrance suits him very well. There is an echo here also of an encounter of Callimachus with the Graces (*Aetia* fr.

7.14–15), who in similar fashion are asked to ensure, in this case by wiping their perfumed hands on his 'elegies', that the poet's work 'last for many a year'.

A poem so concerned with Roman religious festivals requires the reader to pay close attention to the cityscape of Rome, and we have seen some examples of this already. Just as the *Metamorphoses* was as much a poetic map as a world history, so this poem is concerned with space as well as time. The *Mirabilia Urbis Romae*, a late-medieval guidebook to Rome, naturally cites the *Fasti* as a source: 'on the summit of the citadel, above the Porticus Crinorum, there was the temple of Jupiter and Moneta, as is found in Ovid's martyrology (!) of the *Fasti*' (24). An illustration of the encouragement Ovid's poem offers its readers to contemplate their immediate surroundings is 1 March (3.259–392), when Ovid investigates the dancing priests known as the Salii and the cult of Jupiter Elicius, explaining them with a story of a battle of wits between Numa and Jupiter, enticed down to earth, that allows the king to expiate a terrifying spate of thunderbolts. When Jupiter arrives, 'It is agreed that the peak of the Aventine summit trembled, | and the ground sank, weighed down by Jupiter's weight' (3.329–30). Gods were conventionally imagined to be heavier than mortals (compare Diana's superlative height), and Jupiter the heaviest of them all, but here the point is more specific. The altar of Jupiter Elicius was located beside a depression that separated one half of the Aventine hill from the other: today the Viale Aventino (and the Number 3 tram route) runs through it. According to Ovid, the Roman landscape preserves the imprint of Jupiter's visit to the priest-king Numa.

The *Fasti* as Ovid left it is unfinished. Although the text at times anticipates that it will reach its twelfth book and December, it only extends as far as the end of June. Ovid clearly worked further on parts of the poem while in exile, but never apparently to extend it beyond Book 6. That said, Ovid's reference to the state of his poem in *Tristia* 2, his long self-defence addressed to Augustus, is strategically ambiguous on the matter of its full extent: 'Six books of Fasti and as many (again?) have I written | and each roll ends with its month. | This work recently written under your name, Caesar, | and dedicated to you, my fate has broken off' (*Tristia* 2.549–52). The implication might be that July to December could readily be added if Ovid was restored to Rome, but we simply cannot say if Ovid had worked on the second half of the year to any significant degree. The length of a calendar poem is preordained to an unusual degree, it is worth saying, in a way that the dimensions of other poems are not: the *Aeneid* doesn't have to be twelve books long, but the *Fasti* does, and that makes the *Fasti* a poem that it is very effective to cut short. The break also falls before two months of special significance to the emperor: he might reasonably anticipate some honorific material from the months of Julius and Augustus. The premature ending that Ovid did give the *Fasti* encodes both an encouragement to the emperor to reverse his banishment and enjoy the benefit of a topic, superficially at least, so congenial to him, and also a reproach for ensuring that a work of such value to Rome was left unfinished.

The close of Book 6 thus represents an intriguing end to a poetic work, both an end and a denial of one. The last day of June is introduced in strikingly contradictory fashion: 'Tomorrow is the birthday of the Kalends of July. | Muses, add the last touches to my undertaking' (6.797). The content of 30 June rehearses many of the *Fasti*'s preoccupations, praising a woman called Marcia who was a cousin of Augustus and close to Ovid's wife. The occasion, though, is the foundation on this date of the temple of 'Hercules of the Muses', which Marcia's father L. Marcius Philippus, Augustus' stepbrother, had recently restored, and Ovid's notice goes no further back into the history of the temple than Philippus' intervention. But as Ovid and his readers were well aware, this cult had strongly Ennian, and equally strongly calendular, associations. The first edition of Ennius' *Annales* seems to have concluded with the creation of the shrine by Ennius' patron M. Fulvius Nobilior, the addition of a portico containing statues of the nine Muses plundered from military campaigns in Greece to an existing temple of Hercules. (The neighbourhood of this temple, we are told at *Ars Amatoria* 3.168, was also the place to go to buy wigs.)

In addition Nobilior's construction contained calendrical *fasti*, painted on a wall, and *fasti* furthermore apparently embellished with explanatory annotations, the first pale anticipation of Ovid's composition. Ennius, as the author of the *Annales*, a comprehensive poetic history of Rome articulated by year, and with deep interests in time that we have already noted, may well

8. Image of the statue of Hercules of the Muses from a coin of Q. Pomponius Musa, 66 BCE.

have helped his patron Nobilior in his efforts to codify Roman time. All of this hinterland makes Hercules of the Muses a richly appropriate figure with whom to wrap up Ovid's calendrical poem, or if we prefer, makes this temple an achingly inappropriate place to mark its unfortunate interruption.

But Hercules of the Muses must also count as one of the very strangest cult figures in Rome. A series of coins from the 1st century BCE, minted by Q. Pomponius Musa, depicted the nine Muses, a pun on his own name, and an image of Hercules (see Figure 8), the lionskin over his head. But the hero's body is sinuous and feminine, and his tell-tale club set to one side as he strums a lyre. It is with this peace-loving, gender-fluid Hercules striking up on the lyre, *increpuitque lyram* (6.812), that the *Fasti* ends. The spirit of the *Fasti* could hardly find a better representative than his superbly compromised heroism.

Chapter 6
Exile poetry

In 8 or 9 CE, at 50 years of age, the most celebrated literary figure in Rome suffered a catastrophe that would shape the remainder of his life and poetry, banished by Augustus to the city of Tomis on the Black Sea—modern Constanţa in Romania. Ovid repeatedly insists that his punishment was not exile, strictly speaking, but a lesser sanction known as *relegatio* which deprived him neither of his citizenship nor his property: his wife remained behind in Rome to protect that property, and he travelled without his family. But if relegation preserved a shred of dignity for an elite Roman male, it also stipulated where Ovid must reside, and prohibited any departure from it. Tomis was a long, long way from Rome (a month by the quickest mail courier; Ovid, not in any hurry, took six months or more to get there) and it was a cultural backwater, by Ovid's account, its origins as a Greek colony diluted by the local 'barbarian' peoples, the Getae and Sarmatians. After Rome—and no poet rejoiced more in the cultural amenities that Rome offered than Ovid did—this was a traumatic change of scene.

Laeta fere laetus cecini, cano tristia tristis, 'In happy times I generally sang happy songs, in sadness I sing sad', Ovid wrote of his exile poetry (*Epistulae ex Ponto* 3.9.35), with an uncharacteristic commitment to literary propriety. Five books of *Tristia*, 'Sad songs', were followed by four more of *Epistulae ex Ponto*, 'Letters from the Black Sea' (henceforth *Pont.*). *Pont.* 1–3 were apparently issued as one collection, and were probably the last poems published by the poet himself: Book 4 is most likely a posthumous collection (though by what process it was circulated is unknown to us). With the exception of *Tristia* 2, a single, book-length self-defence addressed to the emperor, Ovid's exile poetry reverts to the 'Callimachean' form of the *Amores*, multiple short poems in elegiacs (the metre newly justified by its traditional association with mourning). The main development between *Tristia* and *Pont.* is Ovid's formal adoption of a letter format natural to poems sent over a long distance. The *Pont.* marks a departure also by naming the recipients of the poems: in the *Tristia* names are generally suppressed and anxiety expressed about naming his associates, and the effect is to lend the poetry a claustrophobic quality: Ovid suggests a paranoid, suspicious society in Rome where the basic reflexes of friendship (as well as of poetry, with its power to immortalize its subjects), the naming of one's interlocutor, are interrupted. The latter stages of Augustus' reign saw public and private crises for the emperor, and a less tolerant environment, earlier commitments to punish deeds not words (as Tacitus puts it) breaking down. Equally, the impact of the return of named addressees in the *Pont.* is significant, a restoration of mutuality and friendship further enriched by the personality and profession of the addressees: thus C. Vibius Rufinus, addressed in *Pont.* 1.3 and 3.4, seems to have been an authority on trees, plants, and flowers, including for medicinal purposes, and Ovid's poetic letters to him adopt an appropriately medical line in imagery. But the partial reconstruction of social relations in *Pont.*—and the recipients of Ovid's letters are in most cases from the highest stratum of Roman society—also make the poet's irremediable separation from Rome and society the more poignant.

The reasons for Ovid's exile are presented most clearly in *Tristia* 2, his apologia to the emperor: 'two charges, a poem and a mistake', *duo crimina, carmen et error* (207). The poem is the *Ars Amatoria*, condemned as promoting immoral behaviour ('I am

charged with teaching foul adultery with a shameless poem',
Tristia 2.211–12), but the assumption, in recent scholarship at
least, has been that Augustus used the *Ars* as a pretext to divert
attention from the *real* reason, the 'mistake', which was also
embarrassing to the emperor. The point is made that Ovid was
exiled a long time after the appearance of the *Ars*: those three
books and the *Remedia Amoris* are dated on internal grounds
(mainly references made by Ovid to a campaign against the
Parthian Empire in the East) to between 1 BCE and 2 CE. But there
is some reason to believe that the contribution of the *Ars* was not
as negligible as commonly supposed. At the time of Ovid's
banishment Augustus was involved in some significant tightening
of the moral legislation that had been a cornerstone of his
programme of reform, at heart designed to restore Rome after the
crisis of the Civil Wars, and it isn't hard to see Ovid's dispatch to
the furthest reaches of the empire as a powerful way of
underlining a campaign of public morality.

As for the other charge, the *error*, we find ourselves almost
completely in the dark. Ovid refuses to divulge its nature,
although it is fair to say that in the oblique references he regularly
makes to it he also encourages the reader to speculate (and
speculation has run rife since at least the Middle Ages). What we
do gather is that he was an eyewitness to something, that he was
guilty of a lapse not a crime, and that his mistake was
compounded by fear after the event: a plausible theory is that
Ovid witnessed the planning of some kind of plot against the
emperor, and failed to share what he saw with the authorities.

Ovid's surroundings in Tomis are a topic Ovid returns to
compulsively: 'By your command,' he writes to Augustus in *Tristia*
5.2, 'I have come to the featureless shores of the Black | Sea—this
country lies beneath the chilly pole— | and I am not so much
tortured by a climate never free of cold, | or earth forever scorched
by white frost, | or by the fact that the barbarian tongue is
ignorant of a Latin voice, | and Greek speech is overcome by the

sound of Getic, | as that I am surrounded and pressed on all sides by war close at hand | and an inadequate wall scarcely keeps me safe from the enemy. | Peace there is, nevertheless, from time to time, but never confidence in peace: | thus this place either suffers attack, or fears it.' The themes of insecurity, cultural barbarism, the ugliness and infertility of the landscape, and the arctic climate, are a constant refrain. A twist in a later poem (*Pont.* 3.8) has Ovid struggling to identify a gift he can send to a friend from a land he claims lacks all natural resources: he settles in the end on a quiver full of arrows, weapons of war. Above all, this is a place inimical to the composition of the kind of erudite, polished poetry Ovid was known for: *nec uenit ad duros Musa uocata Getas*, 'The Muse does not come at one's call to the rough Getae' (*Pont.* 1.5.12).

There has been a tendency to assume that Ovid is exaggerating the privations of Tomis. Pushkin in the 19th century, in exile in nearby Bessarabia, disputed Ovid's description of the Black Sea climate, at least, pleasantly temperate as it was from the perspective of a Muscovite. Scepticism is also provoked by Ovid's habit of painting his new environment according to literary convention, and it is undoubtedly true that in seeking to convey the rigours of Tomis, in the words of one scholar, 'he represents the barbarian scene in terms of an alien literary code' (Alessandro Barchiesi): he is an elegiac poet lost in an epic world. But while we certainly cannot read Ovid's account of Tomis as documentary fact, conventional imagery is perfectly compatible in this poetic culture with authentic self-expression. In *Tristia* 1, for example, describing his sea journey from Rome to Tomis, Ovid depicts himself as the learned Hellenistic poet, struggling to compose the kind of poetry naturally written in quiet seclusion. Meanwhile the paraphernalia of the epic mode, storm and an angry Jupiter, threatens to overwhelm the fragile craft bearing the poet. Once in Tomis, the archetypal epic artefact, *arma* or weaponry, beset him: 'I who formerly lived a soft life free of struggle, | amid literary interests and the Muses' choir, | am now surrounded by the crash of Getic arms, far from my country: | and much have I suffered at sea, and

9. The inscription of the Histrians, which formerly served as the lid of a well in Constanța.

much on land' (5.3.9–12). Ovid the delicate elegiac poet is forced to play the role of a hero like Aeneas. Ovid thus engineers a generic tension in this poetry as much as he had in his pre-exile work, but within this literary culture depicting an elegiac poet experiencing epic conditions offers a powerful way of conveying a world out of kilter, and an individual enduring punishment that is entirely disproportionate.

Furthermore, independent evidence has recently emerged of quite how unstable conditions were in the environs of Tomis at this time. This is an inscription (see Figure 9, now in the Museum of Constanța) dating to around 15 CE, probably originating from the city of Histria 25 miles north of Tomis. It honours a commander named Q. Iulius Vestalis for protecting the city against the depredations of 'barbarians' from across the Danube. So serious had this threat from the north become, the inscription informs us, that the Histrians had actually formed an intention of abandoning their city entirely and relocating. Vestalis's military achievements, and those of another commander mentioned in the inscription, L. Pomponius Flaccus, are also celebrated by Ovid in *Pont.* 4, and this new evidence is actually a ringing vindication of Ovid's claims. He was not exaggerating when he wrote, 'You will scarcely find in the whole world, believe me, | a land that less enjoys the Augustan peace' (*Pont.* 2.5.17–18).

It is hard to resist wondering why Augustus banished the miscreant poet to this of all locations. He may have wished to deprive him of the cultural resources, the libraries and literary culture, on which his kind of poetry depended—put more bluntly, to shut him up. If Augustus' promotion of a remedy for Rome's recent crises was a narrative of time-honoured morality and conservative values, Ovid's 'amatory arts and ideas' never sat comfortably with Augustan ideology. But Augustus may also have seen a certain justice in consigning this creature of the peace that he had given Rome, a poet who had stubbornly failed to grasp the urgency of Augustus' project of moral reform for maintaining that peace, to a warzone.

The ostensible aim of Ovid's exile poetry is to make the case that his banishment should be rescinded, or increasingly the more qualified plea to be moved to a more tolerable place of exile: by the time of the *Pont.*, four years or so after his exile, he seems to have abandoned hope of ever seeing Rome itself again. The most systematic defence of the *Ars Amatoria* is to be found in *Tristia* 2. How persuasive we find the case he makes there, indeed how genuine we feel Ovid's attempt is at self-exculpation, is at times in serious doubt: can he really not see, for example, that the description of sexual encounters in Ennius or Virgil, or numerous Greek tragedies, is qualitatively different from an erotic teaching manual, however playful in intent? For that matter, can Ovid of all poets be insensitive to the *double entendre* in his reference to the Dido episode in Virgil's *Aeneid*, 'And yet the blessed author of your *Aeneid* | brought "Arms and the man" to a Tyrian bed' (*Tristia* 2.533–4), where both *arma* and *uirum*, 'arms' and 'man', might suggest the male genitalia—an arresting reframing of the first words (and alternative title) of the greatest poetic achievement of Augustan Rome?

Ovid's characterization of his own work in this context is tendentious, too: the *Ars Amatoria* was 'written strictly for prostitutes' (*Tristia* 2.303), a dubious claim. We have seen already his rewriting of the opening of the *Metamorphoses*, changing 'my times' to 'your times' and implying that Augustus, not Ovid himself, was the real endpoint of the poem. Ovid encourages the emperor to gain a more accurate impression of his poetry by having someone read to him 'the short section in which I have brought the work that begins | from the earliest origins of the world down to your times, Caesar' (559–60), referring to the end of the *Metamorphoses* and its praise of Julius Caesar and Augustus himself. There is an implication that the emperor reads little for himself (he suggests elsewhere that the *Ars* was read to the emperor by a malicious third party). But does this dissemble the comparative absence of Augustus from the *Metamorphoses*, or rather, by the emphasis on its brevity, underline it? The impression is often that Ovid's appeal is really aimed over Augustus' shoulder to his loyal, and knowing, readership.

Whatever the status of this plea for repatriation, the contribution of a poem to his exile makes poetry itself a prominent concern of these collections. Ovid enters exile deeply ambivalent about his own remarkable poetic gift. One way of reading the first book of the *Tristia*, written en route to Tomis, is as dramatizing Ovid's doubts about the very act of writing, and his ultimate discovery of its persisting value: in the final poem of *Tristia* 1 he expresses surprise that he has in fact managed to produce a poetry book, but also acknowledges that an art which has caused him deep distress also provides him, in his darkest hour, with consolation: 'I myself marvel that amid such turmoil of mind and sea | my inspiration has not failed. | Whether trance or madness be the proper name for this activity, | by the pains I took all pain has been lightened'

(1.11.9–12). Ovid regularly equates exile to death, and given the impact of banishment on a Roman male's sense of self, this is more than mere rhetoric. But if Ovid still writes poetry, the implication is that he still exists: 'That I live and withstand harsh sufferings, | and exhaustion with the anxious day does not possess me, | this is thanks, Muse, to you', he states in the biographical poem that ends *Tristia* 4 (10.115–17). There is a similar sentiment, and a defiant expression of it, in what has perhaps been the most celebrated poem of the *Tristia*, 3.7, addressed to his stepdaughter (the daughter of his third and current wife) and fellow poet, Perilla. He will live in his poetry as long as Rome, he proclaims: 'My talent is still my companion and my joy: | Caesar could have no jurisdiction over that' (47–8). Rarely has the simple existence of a book carried such significance as *Tristia* 1, arriving in Rome perhaps as much as a year after its author had been banished to the edge of the civilized world, breaking the silence from this most eloquent man and proclaiming his continued existence.

But the ambivalence about his art—the talent that has both destroyed and preserved him—never goes away. In the first poem of *Tristia* 4 the Muse, synonymous with his talent or *ingenium*, is again credited with bringing him comfort, his only dependable companion in exile, but he goes on to compare poetry to a drug, like the lotos flower that gave pleasure to Ulysses' men even as it ruined them. The poetry that Ovid dispatched back to Rome maintained some kind of presence in the city (only the name of Naso is not yet in exile, he quips at *Tristia* 3.4.45), but they are *tacitae uoces* (*Tristia* 5.13.29), voices without speech, as good as an exile can manage but inadequate all the same.

But if Ovid does not, and cannot, respond to exile by abandoning his trademark *color* or poetic style (it is as a poet that he has value, and he is particularly keen in the first book of *Tristia* to remind readers of the poetry he has written in the past), an important argument he makes in his defence is that the *Ars Amatoria* does not reflect his real life and behaviour: 'Believe me, my morals are far removed from my poetry: | my life is respectable, my Muse playful' (*Tristia* 2.353–4). The picture of Ovid that emerges from exile is in fact strikingly respectable, a family man with children and a devoted wife, a man of property whose fall is often described in terms of the collapse of that most Roman institution, the *domus* or family house. From the long last poem of *Tristia* 4 comes much of the information we have on the poet's life, his brother who died young, and his own early political career, stymied when the words of the legal speeches he tried to write insisted on coming out as verse. A poetic epistle to Pompeius Macer, a friend, fellow-poet, and relative by marriage to whom he also addressed one of the poems of the *Amores*, brings reminiscences of a youthful year spent touring the sights of Asia and Sicily: 'often our exchange of talk made the road seem short, | and our words, if you could count them, were more numerous than our steps' (*Pont.* 2.10.35–6). If we learn more of Ovid's ordinary life, paradoxically, once his ordinary life has been curtailed, it is also true that nowhere, inside or outside Ovid's poetry, do we get so vivid an evocation of the sights and sounds of Rome, as Ovid nostalgically recalls them (*Pont.* 1.8.31–8):

> Sometimes I have memories of you, sweet friends,
>   at times thoughts of my daughter and dear wife steal up on me,
> and from my house I return again to the sites of the beautiful city,
>   and my mind sees everything clearly with eyes of its own.
> Now the forums, now the temples, now the theatres faced in marble,
>   now every portico on its levelled grounds comes before me,
> now the grass of the Campus that looks toward the beautiful gardens,
>   the pools and canals and the waters of the Aqua Virgo.

Ovid insists that exile has hobbled his capacity to write good poetry: the 'limp' of the pentameter after the hexameter in the elegiac couplet, the pentameter one foot shorter than the heroic length, is now attributed to the long journey that his elegies have made to reach their readership in Rome (*Tristia* 3.1.11–12). The greatest shortcoming is one he identifies himself in *Pont.*

3.9, a letter to Brutus, a friend only known to us from Ovid's poetry, who has reported to Ovid that his poetry is not well received in some quarters: 'Because these books of mine contain the same thought, Brutus, | you tell me that someone is criticizing my poetry: | nothing but me asking to enjoy a land closer to home, | and saying how dense is the enemy that surrounds me. | Ah, how he seizes on just one of many faults! | If that is my Muse's only shortcoming, it is good.' But Ovid's poetic decline is much more a rhetorical stance than a reality. One effect of his extended existence away from Rome, he claims, is a loss of facility in Latin: *inter Sauromatas ingeniosus eram*, he comments plaintively on his fifth book of *Tristia* (5.1.74), 'My genius is now Sarmatian', a formulation proving in the process that Ovid's genius for Latin expression is quite undimmed.

Perhaps what we least expect from Ovid, but find in the exile poetry, is pathos, and it is again an effect achieved by the poet's high artistry, not in spite of it. The very first poem from exile, *Tristia* 1.1, pursues a tension between the poetry book, which is returning to Rome, and the poet who is forever excluded from it. It ends with a couplet addressed to his book that encapsulates this dilemma: *longa uia est, propera! nobis habitabitur orbis* | *ultimus, a terra terra remota mea*, 'The road is long, make haste! As for me, I shall dwell at the world's | edge, a land far distant from my land.' The word *ultimus* is lost, most effectively, over the edge of the first line, and in the second line Ovid brings the words denoting Rome and Tomis together: he uses the same word, *terra*, 'land', for each, and sets them beside each other. The possibility of contact, both realized and denied, is beautifully conveyed. The *Epistulae ex Ponto*, as letters, can generate a comparably moving effect from the epistolary formulas with which many of them begin. The first two couplets of *Pont.* 2.2, for example, run, 'He who venerated your house from his earliest years, | Naso, exiled to the left-hand shore of the Black Sea, | sends to you, Messalinus, this greeting from the land of unconquered | Getans which he used to offer face to face.' But my translation of the second couplet, especially, does no justice to Ovid's word placement. In Latin it is *mittit ab indomitis hanc, Messaline, salutem,* | *quam solitus praesens est tibi ferre, Getis,* and just two observations on the composition of these gorgeous lines would be how the Latin for 'this greeting', *hanc . . . salutem*, embraces 'Messalinus', and how very long it takes to travel from the word *indomitis*, 'unconquered', to the noun it qualifies, *Getis*, 'the Getae'.

Stepping back from such close reading, larger compositions explore with comparable psychological acuteness themes fundamental to the exile poetry—poetry's power to bridge the gap between exile and Rome, and its inherent limitations. *Pont.* 4.8 is addressed to P. Suillius Rufus, the husband of Ovid's stepdaughter Perilla, but through Suillius Ovid seeks to gain access to Germanicus: the poem can be dated on internal evidence to 14 CE, soon after the death of Augustus, and Germanicus, adoptive son of Tiberius, is now heir apparent to the imperial throne. The poet asks Suillius to take his case to Germanicus, but before long his instructions as to what his son-in-law should say to the prince slide into a direct address to Germanicus, a promise from Ovid to direct all his poetic abilities to Germanicus' cause. Only in the very last couplet does the poem turn back from Germanicus to Suillius, but it is a moment full of pathos: 'That this petition reach the heavenly powers, dear Suillius, | request on behalf of your all-but-father-in-law.' It is as if the poet has abruptly remembered that he is only addressing Germanicus in imagination. Even his connection to Suillius becomes attenuated, no longer definitively his son-in-law, as his actual circumstances reassert themselves. Another note of pessimism is beautifully made early in his address to Germanicus. He has not the resources, after his exile, to raise a temple to Germanicus in return for his help, Ovid acknowledges, but he will use such riches as he has, his poetry, to express his gratitude: *parua quidem fateor pro magnis munera reddi,* | *cum pro concessa uerba salute damus*, 'Small indeed, I confess, is the offering made in return for great benefits, | if I give words in return for a grant of salvation' (35–6). 'Give words' is already a disparaging way of describing poetry, but *uerba dare* is also an expression in Latin meaning 'cheat' or 'swindle'. At moments like these Ovid's disenchantment with his artistic calling, and that entails his whole existence, is shattering.

The *Tristia* and *Epistulae ex Ponto* were not all that Ovid wrote during his decade in Tomis. The *Fasti* was rededicated to Germanicus (himself a poet) from Tomis and extensively rewritten—quite how extensively has been much debated. More controversial still is what degree of finish the *Metamorphoses* had achieved by the time of his banishment, but it is assumed that this poem was essentially complete. There are strong suspicions also, as we have seen, that the double *Heroides* (16–21) are exilic works. But an undisputed product of his banishment, which also has a claim to be the oddest of Ovid's compositions, is the *Ibis*, a 650-line curse poem directed, like a number of the *Tristia* and *Pont.*, at an anonymous enemy working against his interests back in Rome. Ovid asserts that he is imitating Callimachus (55–60), cursing his enemy *quo modo* ('in the manner' as well as 'in the metre') with which Callimachus had attacked *his* adversary, and the title *Ibis* implies the same: Callimachus had also written an *Ibis*, and it was a curse poem like Ovid's, a popular genre in Hellenistic poetry: the ibis stands in for the evildoer because it was considered a bird of unclean habits—as Pliny the Elder delicately puts it (*Natural History* 8.97), 'cleaning itself through that part of its body by which it is most conducive to health that the residue of its food be discharged'. As the title itself suggests, Callimachus' approach, Ovid informs us, involved *ambages*, 'riddles', 'wrapping up poetry in impenetrable stories'.

Sure enough, after a preliminary section setting the scene, Ovid's *Ibis* embarks on a remarkable string of ghastly calamities that he wishes upon his enemy, culled from myth and history and expressed, one per couplet, in the most indirect and erudite terms. Three couplets, out of a total of nearly 200, can illustrate the range of sources Ovid used, and the concision and violence of his

10. A detail of the Farnese Bull, depicting the punishment of Dirce: this seems to be the statue described by Pliny the Elder (*Natural History* 36.34) as belonging to C. Asinius Pollio, and on public display in Ovid's Rome.

expression: 'And over wild mountains may you be dragged by a ravaging bull, | as the arrogant wife of Lycus was dragged. | And what the unwilling rival of her own sister suffered, | may your tongue be cut out and fall before your feet. | Like the composer of the long-delayed Myrrha, ruined by your last name, | may you be discovered in countless parts of the city' (535–40). Ovid alludes to the myths of Dirce and of Philomela, and to a real recent event, the lynching (famously depicted by Shakespeare) of 'Cinna the poet' after he was mistaken for one of the assassins of Caesar who shared his name. Philomela's grisly story we have encountered in the *Metamorphoses*; Dirce was punished for her mistreatment of Antiope by being tied to a bull, and Ovid's contemporaries could see the myth depicted in a statue group displayed in Rome that survives to this day, the so-called Farnese Bull (see Figure 10). Ovid ends by wishing his enemy the very worst fate of all, 'that amid Sarmatian and Getic arrows, | you live and die in these regions'.

The riddling character of the curses is perhaps explained anthropologically by the need to prevent the target understanding and thus undoing the imprecation, but the length and vehemence of Ovid's catalogue of curses, which obey no obvious organizational principle, have also been seen as characterizing the cursing speaker's unbalanced state of mind. Above all, though, the *Ibis* is stunningly erudite poetry, and this cleaving to Callimachean poetics carries its own charge. Banished far from the cultural resources that were the lifeblood of his kind of poetry, Ovid defiantly fires back a composition of astonishing learnedness for his urban readers to decode.

Ovid informs us that the poetry he sent from Tomis was banned from the public libraries of Rome (*Tristia* 3.1.59–82), but it clearly circulated privately; and as already noted, that was the most important way in which literature circulated in Rome. There is nevertheless a special force to the ostensibly conventional gratitude that Ovid expresses to his 'kind reader' (*candidus lector*), at the close of his autobiographical poem *Tristia* 4.10, for the immortality he still believes he will achieve. A striking illustration of the circulation of the *Tristia* at Rome is an inscription (*Corpus Inscriptionum Latinarum* 6.9632) commemorating L. Valerius Aries, freedman of L. Valerius Zabda, a slave trader, which quotes lines 11–12 of *Tristia* 1.11, and indeed allows the corrupt text of the manuscript tradition at this point to be corrected.

In the longer term what has made Ovid's exile poetry one of the most influential parts of his oeuvre is the rarity of a classical poet offering an intimately personal account of estrangement and alienation. In a poem by Derek Walcott, *The Hotel Normandie Pool*, the poet is around 50, Ovid's age at his banishment, newly divorced, disenchanted with the politics of the Caribbean, and in a more profound way doubly exiled, from his origins by his colonial education, 'the lovely Latin lost to all our schools', and from colonial Britain by his origins. But when Ovid, in the guise of a fellow guest, appears by the side of the hotel pool, he provides some consolation:

> When I was first exiled,
> I missed my language as your tongue needs salt,
> in every watery shape I saw my child,
> no bench would tell my shadow 'Here's your place';
> bridges, canals, willow-framed waterways
> turned from my parting gaze like an insult,
> till, on a tablet smooth as the pool's skin,
> I made reflections that, in many ways,
> were even stronger than their origin.

Walcott seems to endorse Ovid's periodic confidence that poetry can in some way triumph over separation. Two further responses to Ovid's exile poetry, dating to almost the same moment but coming from opposite geographical poles of Ovid's lived experience, carry a similar implication. In 1787 Charles-Joseph Lamoral, 7th Prince de Ligne, an Austrian, was accompanying Catherine the Great of Russia on her progress around the newly conquered territory of Crimea. In a letter from Parthenizza, supposedly the site of a temple of Artemis once served as priestess by Iphigenia (a story told by Euripides, and also by Ovid in *Pont.* 3.2), Ligne's thoughts turned to the Roman poet: 'Perhaps it was here that Ovid wrote; perhaps he was seated where I am.' The prince's geography is not as wayward as it seems: Tomis was not precisely located until the 19th century, and candidates before then included locations in Georgia, Poland, and Ukraine, where there is still a small town called Ovidiopol, so christened by Catherine herself. Catherine's progress around Crimea, with its cities 'restored' to their Greek names (Sebastopol, 'Emperor city', for example), and much emphasis on Iphigenia and her brother Orestes, was largely about forging a European identity for Russia grounded in the classical heritage. All Catherine's companions on her visitation, Ligne included, contributed to a reimagining of

Crimea as a Greek space, and to the concomitant promotion of Russia as the 'Third Rome' in succession to Rome and Byzantium. Here, in other words, Ovid's displacement to the Black Sea facilitates a claim to continuity with a distant place and past.

Shortly after Ligne's reverie on the Black Sea coast, in April 1788, Goethe, the greatest of German writers, was taking leave of Rome for the last time. In a passage that concludes *Italian Journey* he recounts his final melancholy days visiting the classical sites of the city, and feeling a compulsion to compose a poem in elegiac couplets to express his feelings. But when he set about trying to compose it, he could only think of Ovid's description of his own departure from Rome, *Tristia* 1.3, and the text ends, not with Goethe's own poem but with the beginning of Ovid's poem, and Goethe's German translation, in Ovid's metre, elegiacs. Goethe's self-identification with the Roman poet, and with Ovid's perspective from exile, is profound: the rift between exile and home that is so fundamental to the *Tristia* and *Epistulae ex Ponto* here represents a classicist's regret for the distance separating him from the classical world. But again Ovid's poetry offers a model for bridging that rift, as he himself imagined in his most optimistic moments, by poetry.

Without himself to record it, we know nothing about the immediate cause of Ovid's death in Tomis, nor exactly when it took place between 17 and 18 CE.

Further reading

The bibliography on Ovid is huge, particularly from the last half-century. Here I append the main English-language scholarship to which this book is indebted.

R. Armstrong, *Ovid and his Love Poetry* (London, 2005).

A. Barchiesi, 'Future Reflexive: Two Modes of Allusion and Ovid's *Heroides*', *Harvard Studies in Classical Philology* 95 (1993), 333–65.

A. Barchiesi, 'Endgames: Ovid's *Metamorphoses* 15 and *Fasti* 6', in D. H. Roberts, F. M. Dunn, and D. P. Fowler (eds), *Classical Closure: Reading the End in Greek and Latin Literature* (Princeton, 1997), 181–208.

A. Barchiesi, *The Poet and the Prince: Ovid and Augustan Discourse* (Berkeley, 1997).

M. Beard, 'A Complex of Times: No More Sheep on Romulus' Birthday', *Proceedings of the Cambridge Philological Society* 33 (1987), 1–15.

J. W. Binns (ed.), *Ovid* (London, 1973).

S. A. Brown, *The Metamorphosis of Ovid: From Chaucer to Ted Hughes* (London, 1999).

S. Casali, '*Quaerenti plura legendum*: On the Necessity of "Reading More" in Ovid's Exile Poetry', *Ramus* 26 (1997), 80–112.

M. Desmond, 'Venus' Clerk: Ovid's Amatory Poetry in the Middle Ages', in Miller and Newlands (2014), 162–73.

S. Dickinson, 'Russia's First "Orient": Characterizing the Crimea in 1787', *Kritika: Explorations in Russia and Eurasian History* 3 (2002), 3–25.

J. Fairweather, 'Ovid's Autobiographical Poem, *Tristia* 4.10', *Classical Quarterly* 37 (1987), 181–96.

R. E. Fantham, 'Ovid, Germanicus and the Composition of the Fasti', *Papers of the Liverpool Latin Seminar* 5 (1985), 243–81 (also in Knox 2006).

D. C. Feeney, '*Si licet et fas est*: Ovid's *Fasti* and the Problem of Free Speech under the Principate', in A. Powell (ed.), *Roman Poetry and Propaganda in the Age of Augustus* (Bristol, 1992), 1–25.

D. C. Feeney, *Caesar's Calendar: Ancient Time and the Beginnings of History* (Berkeley, 2007).

D. P. Fowler, 'First Thoughts on Closure: Problems and Prospects', *Materiali e discussioni* 22 (1989), 75–122.

L. Fulkerson, *The Ovidian Heroine as Author: Reading, Writing, and Community in the Heroides* (Cambridge, 2005).

P. M. Green, 'The Innocence of Procris: Ovid *A.A.* 3.687–746', *The Classical Journal* 75 (1979), 15–24.

P. M. Green, 'Carmen et Error: πρόφασις and αἰτία in the Matter of Ovid's Exile', *Classical Antiquity* 1 (1982), 202–20.

P. R. Hardie, *Ovid's Poetics of Illusion* (Cambridge, 2002).

P. R. Hardie, A. Barchiesi, and S. J. Hinds (eds), *Ovidian Transformations: Essays on Ovid's Metamorphoses and its Reception* (Cambridge, 1999).

S. J. Heyworth, '*Ars Moratoria* (Ovid, *AA* 1.681–704)', *Liverpool Classical Monthly* 17 (1992), 59–61.

S. E. Hinds, 'Booking the Return Trip: Ovid and *Tristia* 1', *Proceedings of the Cambridge Philological Society* 31 (1985), 13–32 (also in Knox 2006).

S. E. Hinds, *The Metamorphosis of Persephone: Ovid and the Self-conscious Muse* (Cambridge, 1987).

S. E. Hinds, 'Arma in Ovid's *Fasti*, Part 1: Genre and Mannerism', *Arethusa* 25 (1992), 81–112.

A. S. Hollis, 'The Ars Amatoria and Remedia Amoris', in Binns (1973), 84–115.

N. Holzberg, '*Ter quinque volumina* as *carmen perpetuum*: The Division into Books in Ovid's *Metamorphoses*', *Materiali e discussioni* 40 (1998), 77–98.

J. M. Horowitz, 'Ovid in Restoration and Eighteenth-Century England', in Miller and Newlands (2014), 355–70.

G. O. Hutchinson, 'Some New and Old Light on the Reasons for Ovid's Exile', *Zeitschrift für Papyrologie und Epigraphik* 203 (2017), 76–84.

J. Ingleheart (ed.), *Two Thousand Years of Solitude: Exile after Ovid* (Oxford, 2011).

C. Jameson, 'Ovid in the Sixteenth Century', in Binns (1973), 210–11.

G. Kantor, 'The Date and Circumstances of Quintus Iulius Vestalis', *Zeitschrift für Papyrologie und Epigraphik* 203 (2017), 85–91.

A. M. Keith, *Engendering Rome: Women in Latin Epic* (Cambridge, 2000).

D. F. Kennedy, 'The Epistolary Mode and the First of Ovid's *Heroides*', *The Classical Quarterly* 34 (1984), 413–22 (also in Knox 2006).

E. J. Kenney, 'A Byzantine Version of Ovid', *Hermes* 91 (1963), 213–27.

E. J. Kenney, 'Ovid and the Law', *Yale Classical Studies* 21 (1969), 243–63.

E. J. Kenney, 'Love and Legalism: Ovid, *Heroides* 20 and 21', *Arion* 9 (1970), 388–414.

P. E. Knox (ed.), *Oxford Readings in Ovid* (Oxford, 2006).

E. W. Leach, 'Georgic Imagery in the *Ars Amatoria*', *Transactions and Proceedings of the American Philological Association* 95 (1964), 142–54.

J. C. McKeown, 'Augustan Elegy and Mime', *Proceedings of the Cambridge Philological Society* 25 (1979), 71–84.

C. Martindale (ed.), *Ovid Renewed: Ovidian Influences on Literature and Art from the Middle Ages to the Twentieth Century* (Cambridge, 1988).

J. F. Miller, *Ovid's Elegiac Festivals: Studies in the Fasti* (Frankfurt am Main, 1991).

J. F. Miller, 'Ovid's *Fasti* and the Neo-Latin Christian Calendar Poem', *International Journal of the Classical Tradition* 10 (2003), 173–86.

J. F. Miller and C. E. Newlands, *A Handbook to the Reception of Ovid* (Chichester, 2014).

Ll. Morgan, 'Child's Play: Ovid and his Critics', *Journal of Roman Studies* 93 (2003), 66–91.

Ll. Morgan, 'Ovid, *Fasti* 3.330', *Classical Quarterly* 64 (2014), 855–9.

T. Nelson, '"Most Musicall, most Melancholy": Avian Aesthetics of Lament in Greek and Roman Elegy', *Dictynna* [Online] 16 (2019), online since 29 November 2019, connection on 20 December 2019. <http://journals.openedition.org/dictynna/1914>.

W. S. M. Nicoll, 'Cupid, Apollo and Daphne (Ovid, Metamorphoses 1.452ff.)', *Classical Quarterly* 30 (1980), 174–82.

E. Oliensis, 'Return to Sender: The Rhetoric of *nomina* in Ovid's *Tristia*', *Ramus* 26 (1997), 172–93.

M. Pasco-Pranger, *Founding the Year: Ovid's Fasti and the Poetics of the Roman Calendar* (Leiden, 2006).

S. B. Pomeroy, *Whores, Wives, and Slaves: Women in Classical Antiquity* (New York, 1975).

E. K. Rand, *Ovid and his Influence* (Boston, 1925).

D. M. Robathan, 'Ovid in the Middle Ages', in Binns (1973), 191–209.

M. Robinson, 'Ovid, the *Fasti* and the Stars', *Bulletin of the Institute of Classical Studies* 50 (2007), 129–59.

A. R. Sharrock, 'Womanufacture', *Journal of Roman Studies* 81 (1991), 36–49.

J. D. Solodow, *The World of Ovid's Metamorphoses* (Chapel Hill, NC, 1988).

H. Taylor, *The Lives of Ovid in Seventeenth-Century French Culture* (Oxford, 2017).

G. Tissol, *The Face of Nature: Wit, Narrative, and Cosmic Origins in Ovid's Metamorphoses* (Princeton, 1997).

G. D. Williams, 'Representations of the Book-roll in Latin Poetry: Ovid, *Tr.* 1.1.3–14 and Related Texts', *Mnemosyne* 45 (1992), 178–89.

G. D. Williams, *The Curse of Exile: A Study of Ovid's Ibis* (Cambridge, 1996).

Index

For the benefit of digital users, indexed terms that span two pages (e.g., 52–53) may, on occasion, appear on only one of those pages.

Ovid

Index

V

W

Ovid

CLASSICAL MYTHOLOGY
A Very Short Introduction
Helen Morales

From Zeus and Europa, to Diana, Pan, and Prometheus, the myths of ancient Greece and Rome seem to exert a timeless power over us. But what do those myths represent, and why are they so enduringly fascinating? This imaginative and stimulating *Very Short Introduction* is a wide-ranging account, examining how classical myths are used and understood in both high art and popular culture, taking the reader from the temples of Crete to skyscrapers in New York, and finding classical myths in a variety of unexpected places: from Arabic poetry and Hollywood films, to psychoanalysis, the bible, and New Age spiritualism.

www.oup.com/vsi

ENGLISH LITERATURE
A Very Short Introduction
Jonathan Bate

Sweeping across two millennia and every literary genre, acclaimed scholar and biographer Jonathan Bate provides a dazzling introduction to English Literature. The focus is wide, shifting from the birth of the novel and the brilliance of English comedy to the deep Englishness of landscape poetry and the ethnic diversity of Britain's Nobel literature laureates. It goes on to provide a more in-depth analysis, with close readings from an extraordinary scene in King Lear to a war poem by Carol Ann Duffy, and a series of striking examples of how literary texts change as they are transmitted from writer to reader.

{No reviews}

www.oup.com/vsi

FRENCH LITERATURE
A Very Short Introduction
John D. Lyons

The heritage of literature in the French language is rich,
varied, and extensive in time and space; appealing both to its
immediate public, readers of French, and also to aglobal
audience reached through translations and film adaptations.
French Literature: A Very Short Introduction introduces this lively
literary world by focusing on texts - epics, novels, plays, poems,
and screenplays - that concern protagonists whose adventures
and conflicts reveal shifts in literary and social practices. From
the hero of the medieval *Song of Roland* to the Caribbean
heroines of *Tituba, Black Witch of Salem* or the European
expatriate in Japan in *Fear and Trembling*, these problematic
protagonists allow us to understand what interests writers and
readers across the wide world of French.

www.oup.com/vsi

GERMAN LITERATURE
A Very Short Introduction
Nicholas Boyle

German writers, from Luther and Goethe to Heine, Brecht, and Günter Grass, have had a profound influence on the modern world. This *Very Short Introduction* presents an engrossing tour of the course of German literature from the late Middle Ages to the present, focussing especially on the last 250 years. Emphasizing the economic and religious context of many masterpieces of German literature, it highlights how they can be interpreted as responses to social and political changes within an often violent and tragic history. The result is a new and clear perspective which illuminates the power of German literature and the German intellectual tradition, and its impact on the wider cultural world.

'Boyle has a sure touch and an obvious authority...this is a balanced and lively introduction to German literature.'

Ben Hutchinson, TLS